Oh $h*t! I'm Getting Divorced.
The Guide to Keeping Your Dignity and Dollars

Paperback ISBN: 978-1-947276-24-6
eBook ISBN: 978-1-947276-23-9
ASIN: B09WXGVB3B

Publishing and Design:

EPIC AUTHOR
PUBLISHING

Ordering Information: Exclusive discounts for quantity purchases.

Contact: info@bridgingllc.com | www.bridgingdivorcesolutions.com

First Edition

Oh $h*t! I'm getting divorced

The Guide To Keeping Your Dignity And Dollars

Brenda Bridges
CDFA®, CDC®, RICP®, MAT

DEDICATION

TO MY AMAZING CHILDREN. You are the strongest, kindest, and most talented humans I know.

Thank you for your love, patience, and understanding. You guys keep me grounded and centered, reminding me of what truly matters in life. You inspire me every day.

Love you to the moon and back.

TABLE OF CONTENTS

FOREWORD

GOING INTO MARRIAGE, divorce wasn't a club you ever envisioned yourself joining. You weren't going to be a statistic. Yet, here you are, holding a copy of *Oh $h*T! I'm Getting Divorced.*

If you haven't already, sooner or later, reality will hit, and you will have your Oh $h*t! moment. Here's what you need to know; there's more to divorce than simply dividing assets. Personally, I wish I'd had Brenda's wisdom bestowed on me when I was divorcing. For me, it was a math equation. In hindsight, I could have benefited from her non-traditional approach, and I hope you give this way of divorcing a try.

What you are about to discover is that there's hope for a brighter, better future, and the whole process doesn't have to be the worst experience of your life. Brenda provides alternatives to vindictive divorce.

You know, the kind where you hear, or perhaps, you say things like:

"She's not getting my money."

"Take him for all he's got."

"I've got more money than she does, so I'll drag this out."

"He did you wrong. Make him pay for it."

"He's never going to see the kids again."

*Oh $h*t! I'm Getting Divorced* is a different and meaningful way of dissolving your marriage.

Meaningful? Yes, if you are open to outside-the-box ways of thinking. Mindfully balancing emotions and finances is a unique approach that Brenda will guide you through.

Sound unusual? That's because it is. And it's why it resonates so well with me. Brenda's process is unconventional as she teaches you to find your power and to consider your next steps---today, tomorrow, and years down the road. You don't have to settle. You have options. You can avoid defaulting on your financial future, and you don't have to endure emotional bankruptcy. Instead of focusing on "winning" your divorce, what would it look like to think ahead to what's next in your life?

Give serious consideration to how you want to feel post-divorce. Chances are, you've witnessed the nightmares of friends' divorces. While divorce isn't a wonderful experience, it can be less ugly when you get an expert involved.

I've been fortunate to have Brenda as my business accountability partner for years. I trust her, love her heart, and appreciate her unique perspective. She has both personal and professional expertise to help guide you in your divorce.

Consider this, to help you divorce better than she did, Brenda committed to getting educated in the subject of divorce. She invested her time learning and earning multiple credentials to serve YOU! Not only that, as an investment professional, she has extensive knowledge pertaining to different types of assets and associated tax implications and is equipped to help you understand your post-divorce income strategy. She's seen the good, the bad, and the ugly and can help you have a "good divorce."

I believe books are great resources; however, they can't give you advice specific to your situation, nor can they hold you accountable. I'm confident that when you hire Brenda to help you navigate the hurdles you will face in your divorce, you will get heartfelt guidance, expert advice, and accountability to divorce with your dignity and your dollars.

Warmly,

—Melissa Myers, CFP®
Wealth Manager
#1 Best Selling Author Going Rogue!
Unconventional Financial Strategies for Women

Testimonial statements made by Brenda, a peer of Brenda may not be representative of the experience of other customers and are no guarantee of future performance or success.

A NOTE ABOUT THE TITLE

THIS BOOK TITLE STARTED out as "divorce with dignity and grace."

You probably won't be surprised to find that DID NOT resonate with people who suddenly find their "happily ever after" is headed to court, and they don't have a clue what to do next.

And so, we set about finding out what DID. Turns out swearing resonates. The choice of swear words might be different, but the initial sentiment is the same.

The first feeling when reality sinks in and people realize what they're up against as they move forward unmarried is definitely "Oh, shit!"

The purpose of this book is to shine a light on *that* moment and help you move from a deer in headlights to an educated human who can make their own informed decisions. This is to help you know what to do next. For YOU. The first step is recognizing where you are at the beginning.

It begins with "Oh, shit!"

The rest of the book helps you figure out what to do next.

> Let us make our future now and let us make our dreams tomorrow's reality.
> —Malala Yousafzai

MESSAGE TO THE READER

"You will either step forward into growth or backward into safety."
—Abraham Maslow

THE NEWS OF MY DIVORCE was delivered by my then-husband after his usual early morning Starbucks run. He cruised into the kitchen as I sat at the table doing some busy work on my laptop before leaving for the day. He took a swig of his venti dark roast, leaned against the island, and made the announcement that changed all of our lives. It went something like this . . .

"I was going to write you a letter, but I figured I should tell you in person," he said.

I'm thinking that's odd—why would he write me a letter when we're both right here. He's not usually one to write me anything. Is it an idea or guest list for my upcoming birthday? My fiftieth was just weeks away, I thought we were going to have a bowling party.

"I'm done. There's no glue. I'm not doing therapy—it doesn't work. Now, go to work."

Definitely not a party. In shock, I did what he said. I got in my car, called my best friend, and repeated what just happened.

And, as I cried, I wondered what was next.

For our family, next was wading through what I believe to be a needlessly expensive and damaging process. I wish I could say I did it really well and that's why I'm writing this book.

Nope. I did not do it well. I crumbled. I drank too much. I didn't sleep. I lost a ton of weight. I worried incessantly about the great unknown that was coming and how to figure out what to do next. I was not a good mom. I was barely a functioning human.

My divorce, in so many ways, was my undoing. And it is also what led me to my purpose.

I want to help you have a different experience.

> I don't see divorce as a failure. I see it as the end of a story. In a story, everything has an end and a beginning. —Olga Kurylenko

I know, in my heart, if I'd had access to different resources and support in the months and years that followed instead of getting swept up in the drama, trauma, and intrigue our society accepts as the divorce process, we would all have been better off.

I wrote this book to provide you with the roadmap to the process I was looking for years ago. One that both takes into account the factual, logical decisions you need to make and acknowledges the very real stress and grief coloring those decisions, both at exactly the same time.

Divorce is one of the most stressful life events a person can go through.[1]

1 "Where Are You on the Divorce Stress Scale?" *Psychology Today*, Sussex Publishers, https://www.psychologytoday.com/us/blog/contemplating-divorce/201207/where-are-you-the-divorce-stress-scale.

It's difficult, expensive, and emotionally exhausting.

Without the proper support, my divorce spiraled into an incredibly expensive, drawn-out shit show. More on that later. I didn't want that for myself, and I don't want it for you.

I knew, after going through that, there had to be a better way.

I was already a financial advisor, but a newly minted one because I'd just started that career the year prior to the divorce news rocking my world. I couldn't help but think if I understand finances better than the average bear and still ended up in this mess, what happens to people who don't? Where's the information for divorcing couples on how you streamline the process, acknowledge the difficulty and loss while focusing on the future to get the best outcome for you and your family?

My own journey, along with years of experience working with divorcing couples as they figure out financial agreements and co-parenting, leads me to believe firmly that much of the damage can be avoided with the right information, good "thought partners," and the right professional support.

In these pages, I share resources I searched for and couldn't find during my divorce. Facts about processes that can save you a lot of money and heartache. I also want you to feel supported and acknowledged for working through decisions you will be asked to make, decisions that are not all logical and straightforward.

You're not alone.

Warmly,

Brenda

INTRODUCTION

Don't spend time beating on a wall,
hoping it will transform into a door.
—Coco Chanel

WHAT TO EXPECT

There Are Two Schools of Thought about Approaching Divorce.

There's a side that encourages you to check your emotions at the door and make all your decisions as if you were entirely logical.

They advocate getting your facts straight and making practical decisions. This view emphasizes the financial piece, as though your marriage was a business venture with no emotional impact. They would advise learning the facts about the divorce rules in their jurisdiction, the equation used to determine support, or dividing assets in settlements. Throw your life into a spreadsheet, do a sort on the columns, and presto, easy-peasy decisions are made.

Sounds good, but this is unrealistic; it's not how humans operate.

The other side is working on the emotional support needed in this enormous life transition.

How do you address your feelings? How do you deal with and heal from the fallout of your experience? If you're a parent, you're probably responsible for your children and their emotions.

There are all shapes and sizes of books dealing with divorce's mental and emotional stress—from narcissistic gaslighting to high-conflict relationships.

Introducing a third option . . .

What if we recognize the business-like decisions about finances, schedules, and assets while acknowledging the layers upon layers of feelings that impact our rational choices?

As much as we'd like to consider ourselves logical beings, emotion drives our decision-making.[2] As divorce is one of the most highly emotional events you can experience, it's just plain silly to think you'll be in an excellent place to make logical decisions without information and coaching through the process.

What if you are guided by a process that coaches you to make the best choices *for you*?

A process that saves you time, money, and conflict encouraged by the court system.

---

2 Whitener, Svetlana. "Council Post: How Your Emotions Influence Your Decisions." *Forbes*, Forbes Magazine, 12 Oct. 2022, https://www.forbes.com/sites/forbescoachescouncil/2018/05/09/how-your-emotions-influence-your-decisions/.

Instead of thinking of your journey like this:

What if we recognize the pattern is more like this:

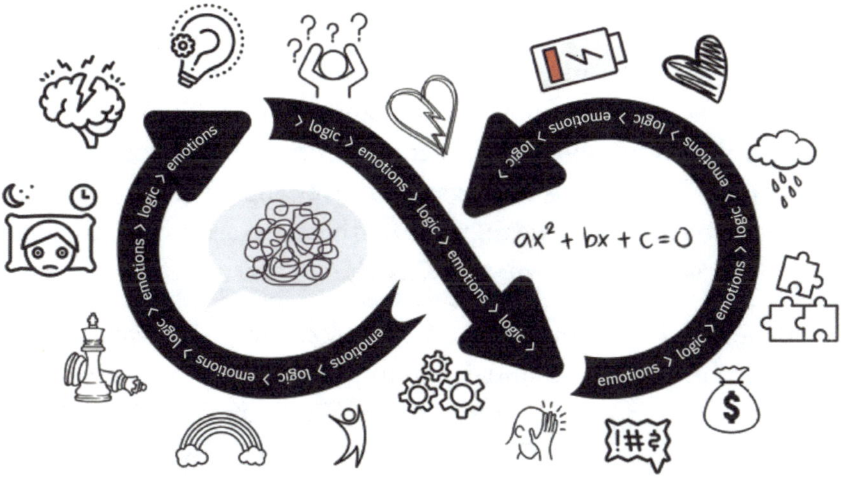

I'll be your coach and advisor through the beginning stages of the divorce process. I'll provide the information you need so you're equipped to make better decisions without the expectation of making decisions like an emotionless robot.

WHY LISTEN TO ME?

You know why I landed in this space. My divorce was a messed up, expensive, damaging shit show.

I want to stop that from happening to you and your family. At the very minimum, I want to help make it suck less.

I had some learning to do.

My first step was to study the financial aspect of divorce. The year after my divorce was complete, I became a Certified Divorce Financial Analyst® (CDFA).[3] That certification program is dedicated to the intricacies of money decisions in divorce, much of it geared toward giving people accurate information to make financial decisions and avoid mistakes.

After practicing in that area, it became evident that there was a missing link. Lawyers know the law, and CDFAs® know the money matters, but what about the feelings driving the decisions? All this financial information is important but overwhelming. Sometimes it is even presented in a vacuum. Sure, there are a lot of good numbers—but what do they mean? Why should you care?

Believing that people make better decisions with accurate and useful information and understanding the *why* behind their behaviors, I continued my "all things divorce" education by becoming a Certified Divorce Coach® (CDC)[4] and Certified Divorce Transition and Recovery Coach®. Coaching added the missing piece. With helpful coaching, we work through choices in the framework of our individual stories and the baggage we likely carry out of the mar-

3 "Working with a CDFA." *IDFA*, https://institutedfa.com/learning-center/what-cdfa-professional/.

4 Squinx. "CDC Board of Standards." Certified Divorce Coach®, n.d. https://certifieddivorcecoach.com/cdc-board-of-standards/.

riage. This skill set helps acknowledge emotions without being ruled by them.

With a master's degree in teaching, I was already an educator.

I also became a trained mediator, sprinkling in sensibilities from yoga, where I hold the 500-hour instructor's certification.

I'm a Financial Advisor, Certified Divorce Coach, Certified Divorce Financial Analyst, Divorce Transition Coach, and Divorce Mediator. I help people with all the non-legal parts of a divorce. Especially understanding the financial realities.

While no two divorces are the same, as no two marriages are the same, I think the most important credential I offer is that I've gone through my own divorce and came out wiser, stronger, and happier. Since then, I've made it my life's work to help others do that, too.

THIS BOOK IS FOR YOU IF

You (or your spouse) have decided you want a divorce and need to figure out the next best step; this book can save you money and missteps. You will find information that helps you in the "you don't know what you don't know" arena. Some portions of this book may be incredibly pertinent to you; some may not seem so at the time but things pop up.

What this book isn't. This book isn't a discernment aid. It's not intended to help you figure out if divorce is the choice you want to make. It's intended to help you make the right choices after you've decided to divorce.

As you start the process, we'll walk through getting clear on your choices, considering both your feelings and the facts.

Finish this book, and you should have a framework to:

- Understand your options and match them to your situation (yes, you have choices!)
- Get organized, know the information you need and why
- Set yourself up to stay goal focused, clearly frame your decisions by balancing emotion and logic
- Save you time, money, and misunderstandings

Realize that how you start is going to drive how everything else plays out. If you dive into divorce raging and vengeful, the chances of that settling down in the months and potentially years it takes to complete the process are slim. You may have every right and reason to be angry, and while feeding the anger might feel good short term, in the long run, it can be more damaging to you than it is to anyone else.

BONUS, YOU LEARN A NEW LANGUAGE

Understandably this is a bonus you could do without. You'll find divorce has a language of its own. Even the most conscientious professionals can fall into the trap of speaking in acronyms or jargon as though you understand what we're saying.

A secret decoder ring would be more fun. Instead, you can use a glossary in the back of the book to translate if a case of legal-ease or financial jargon sets in.

And, of course, ask! If you have the right team of professionals, they should be more than willing to explain what they're talking about.

HOW TO USE OH $H*T! I'M GETTING DIVORCED: THE GUIDE TO KEEPING YOUR DIGNITY AND DOLLARS

You can use this book traditionally, starting at the beginning and working through to the end. This order might be beneficial if you're just beginning the process. Walking through the decisions, journaling about them, and understanding your options WILL leave you better off than if you only let the system pick you up and carry you along in its current.

You can also use this book as a reference if you find yourself midstream and want to get information, support, and guidance in thinking through your situation. In this case, jump to the chapter or chapters that address the issues you are dealing with. Take the information provided here to contemplate your situation and your choices.

I divide the book into three sections.

Part I. Frame of Mind

Part II. Family and Friends

Part III. Finances and Logistics

A check-in between each part gives you a gentle reminder to revisit your "why" as you move through the process.

Your "why" in divorce refers to the purpose or motivation behind the decisions made during the process. Your "why" is the reason behind every decision and action you take. Your "why" is based on what you want your life to look like after your divorce is complete. A clear understanding of your "why" can help guide you in making informed and confident choices, provide clarity in navigating complex and emotional issues, and ensure that your actions align with your values and priorities. Knowing your "why" can make the divorce process smoother and produce a better outcome, helping you move forward in a positive direction. Sometimes losing track of what's behind your decisions can lead to decisions that are not true to what you want.

Part I. **Frame of Mind**

The first part of this book helps you dig deeper into what you want for your future, investigate the options, and plan to move forward. Your initial plan might get derailed even if you approach your divorce thoroughly and thoughtfully. That is the way of the family law court system (one in desperate need of change, but that's another book).

The more you know about your options, the more equipped you are to stand for what you want and think is right, and the less likely you are to accept it when you hear things like "that's just the way we do it here." I don't want you to fall for that trap (or crap, depending on your point of view). This is your life. Approaching it with intent makes it much more likely you will have a satisfactory outcome.

You will develop your "why" in Part I: Frame of Mind. It's essential that you revisit it as you move through the process. You may find it shifts, or you may find it is your North Star, reminding you to keep focused on what you know to be right for you and not get bogged down in minutia.

Part II. **Family and Friends**

Part II is for those of you who have children or want some support for navigating divorce in your social circles and extended family.

These chapters address practical matters like what to consider as you develop your parenting plan. Part II also discusses how your extended family and social life might be upended in your divorce, so you can think about how you'd like that to look post-divorce.

Besides "I kept the friends" being the source of dark humor, we should discuss it. I know, nothing in the court system or formal divorce process addresses "who gets the friends."

Part III. **Finances and Logistics**

In Part III, you get grounded in your options and understand the nature of the financial decisions you must address. This is when you get honest with yourself about what you can expect and your financial goals and then circle back to the "why" roadmap you worked on in Part I.

Working through this section, you will learn what you didn't realized you needed to know and where you need more information. You'll get savvy about the realities you face post-divorce. You will make better decisions. No one else. You are the boss of you. You decide what you do and why. Do it with accurate, complete information, and don't let yourself get pushed into a situation you don't understand or haven't investigated thoroughly.

I will coach you to consider other options, don't spend years of your life and potentially tens of thousands (or hundreds of thousands) of dollars if the cost far outweighs the potential benefits. In Part III, I examine options, clear up misconceptions, and lay out a roadmap for you to make well-informed decisions.

PART I:
FRAME OF MIND

CHAPTER 1

Where to Start

Stay committed to your decisions,
but stay flexible in your approach.
—Tony Robbins

THE SINGLE MOST COMMON COMMENT I hear in my first call with a potential client is, "I don't know what to do. I don't know where to start."

My most frequent response is, here is where you **don't** start.

Don't start with the conditioned first step, hiring an attorney. This is the stuff of TV shows and social hearsay. As is the dramatic play "you've been served."

Legal representation is essential, divorce is a legal process, and potentially much is at stake. You want to ensure you have the proper representation for yourself and your rights.

That being said, going straight to hiring an attorney is jumping the gun in the majority, the vast majority, of cases.

Depending on your circumstances, hiring an attorney may be exactly the right thing and best choice for you. It's still not the first step.

The first step is to think beyond the end of your marriage and have clarity about what you want your life, and if you are a parent, your children's lives, to look like post-divorce.

DON'T DO DIVORCE LIKE EVERYONE ELSE.

Being mindful of what you want can be crazy hard and can take significant follow-through. Working through your baggage and separating what you want from what you're used to saying or doing will pay off in the long run.

Sometimes being mindful can look good without doing any good. Does this resonate with you? Truth be told, I often do it myself.

So what does mindfulness look like?

A perfectly safe space where I sit, get centered, and take pen to paper. I've lit a candle beside me, brewed a cup of tea, and opened the windows to hear the birds. I open my journal with thick, pebbled pages and inspirational quotes. I begin.

I think, and I dream. Maybe I cry. Mindfully, I map out my vision of the future. It's based on good intentions and thoughtfulness. I put my heart and soul into it. After all, I've set aside this time to go deep and figure out what I want this life to look like; I should do it with complete conviction.

This exercise is not meant to set goals crafted around having things. I shape my vision around being true to myself and those I love on how to serve others with what I've learned so far. When we put our intentions into the universe, it starts working for us regardless of our conscious minds.

And then I tuck away the journal and get occupied with whatever busy thing I'm doing. Life needs living, dinner needs making, and plants need planting. Reports must be completed, bills must be paid, and applications must be filled out.

And my vision takes a back seat to life.

It's not always easy to put words to your vision, and it can be hard to stick to it when life gets in the way. And, as you move through the process, your vision may also shift. Things you feel are critical initially may fall away, and other things take their place on your list of priorities or **dreams**.

It's the most essential first step and will help guide you in the right direction to decide what process to use and what's vital for your outcome. And, just as important, keep revisiting your vision as you walk through new decisions to see if you still want the same thing. If you're veering off course, figure out what needs attention. Do you need to revise your vision, or do you need to revise your actions?

I started my divorce process with the mantra of going through it with grace and dignity. If you read the introduction, perhaps you'll remember that it was initially the title of this book. I'd go to my then church, walk the labyrinth they had set up for Lent, and repeat to myself, "grace and dignity." Grace and dignity. Dignity and grace.

Had I written goals down then, it would have been those two words and those two words alone. As things progressed and we got deeper into the process, it got angrier, uglier, more expensive, and more out of control. My mantra got lost, and so did I.

I left grace and dignity behind to pour another glass of Chardonnay and wish the whole thing would disappear. I am not proud of that. I had spent years perfecting the art of making things look good to other people. I couldn't do it anymore, yet I didn't know how else to be. I was collapsing on the inside.

I'd spent many years making it appear all was fine, beyond fine, extraordinary. We had it all. Brilliant children, two houses, a country club, and cute dogs. And it was not a happy place. And as my house of cards collapsed, people would say things like, "this can't be happening to you; you have everything." I crumbled. And I tried to keep up with expectations of doing all the family things I had before, building a career at age fifty, getting through the divorce, making some of the most challenging decisions I'd ever faced, and figuring out where I'd packed away my backbone and joy.

Once, I was riding the wave of crazy that can be divorce; it impacted my and my children's lives in ways I never anticipated.

It was devastating to my kids. They were going through their own divorce experience and losing the family and lifestyle they'd known. I was running on fumes and headed to empty.

That phase did a number on my health. I got caught up in extreme depression and anxiety. I lost a ton of weight, then gained all that and more back. I was stressed to the point of not wanting to get up another day and couldn't sleep at night. I'd stay up and make cold call lists for a job that was crushing me. Or lose nights in the fog of trying to escape with alcohol. After never having severe health issues, my cholesterol was sky-high. I was in a constant state of stress. I stopped exercising regularly, formerly a routine part of my world and lost almost all of my social network, which had been my support system, even if it was on a surface level.

It wasn't a pretty picture, and I carry a lot of shame. I still think about how I handled myself and how it affected my ability to be there for my children.

I try to maintain compassion for my past self and focus on the world it opened for me moving forward.

After all, that low place shaped my passion for helping others like you avoid my mistakes. At the time, I desperately needed to be held, not physically, but by someone having space for me on this incredibly stressful emotional journey with the specter of a financial sinkhole around every corner. I wanted not to be alone. To be seen and understood.

I didn't know what I needed until I experienced a small but significant turning point.

This turning point shook me out of my destructive path and helped me make small but powerful decisions that put me on the path to healthier healing.

I GOT A NEW MANTRA. RADICAL ACCEPTANCE.

One of my greatest wishes is that by reading this now and maybe revisiting it if it serves you, you'll be encouraged to avoid that destructive path that may cause damage to yourself and others. I'm here to tell you that it's OK to not be OK. Divorce can be traumatic. Studies even say it's more devastating a loss than death for children and second only to the death of a spouse for adults.[5]

5 "The Healthy Journal - Gluten, Dairy, Sugar Free Recipes, Interviews and Health Articles," n.d. https://www.thehealthyjournal.com/faq/what-hurts-more-divorce-or-death.

According to the Holmes-Rahe Life Stress Inventory, divorce comes in second behind the death of a spouse as one of the most stressful situations people may go through. In addition, research suggests people who experience a significant life event such as divorce are 2.5 to 9.4 times more likely to develop depression.[6]

Let me walk you back to the night that was my first turning point. I'm a year into an out-of-control, costly divorce process, which I don't understand or feel supported. Most friends or social support I'd enjoyed for decades have fallen away.

One kind woman invited me to a party, saying you'll meet many people who can support you because they are just like you. Just like me. I felt like an alien in my own body. I was curious about what these other divorcée life forms were like.

I pull myself together. I style my hair, put on make-up, and dress as if I care about how I present myself. I got in my little car and drove myself to the party alone. I genuinely remember feeling like I did when I was twelve and we moved to a new city. "Please like me. Please like me. Please like me. At least don't make fun of me." My fragile self-esteem is so low I don't think it can take another blow.

I park. Checking the rearview mirror to ensure my mascara hadn't turned me into a raccoon, I make sure I am at the right house, walk up to the door, and knock. No

6 "The Healthy Journal - Gluten, Dairy, Sugar Free Recipes, Interviews and Health Articles," n.d. https://www.thehealthyjournal.com/faq/is-divorce-worse-than-death.

answer. Knock and knock. No answer. Phew, there's my opening to get out of here. Maybe I should turn around and return home; this is exhausting. But there is a beacon of hope that women like me are in this house. After my divorce's initial novelty and intrigue, most friends I spent time with moved back into their lives without me. I didn't fit there anymore.

So I straightened my shoulders, opened the door, and walked in. About twenty women talk, laugh, and drink; no one notices as I enter. It's that awkward moment, assess the situation and figure out what to do next. Grab a drink and hold on to it for security? Boldly walk into a cluster of women and introduce myself? Things I wouldn't have hesitated to do two or three years earlier leave me frozen.

Luckily, the woman who invited me spots me and walks me over to a group of women engrossed in conversation. It goes something like this:

"Brenda, meet Jeannie. Jeannie's been divorced for two years."

"Hi, Jeannie." Shaky smile. Is she my new friend?

"Brenda, meet Leila. Leila's been divorced for seven years, but they're back in court."

"Hey Leila, good to meet you." Back in court? Are you kidding?

"Brenda, this is Sam; she's just like you. She's going through divorce now, maybe a few months ahead."

Internal sigh. Sam! Maybe Sam is my new friend and support sister.

"Hi Sam, it's terrific to meet you."

The rest of the conversation went like this; "So. Brenda, who is your attorney?" "What is your dickhead husband doing?" "How much are you going to get in the divorce?" "My attorney is a total asshole; want their name?"

Here is my wake-up call. I am surrounded by people who have decided to relive the wrongs done to them through their divorce. And gather and relive them together.

Even though almost all were divorced, some for years, they were still in that marriage. Not one person in the room said she was better after her divorce.

This evening was not my beacon of hope or how I wanted to end up.

I didn't find what I was looking for that night.

Something found me that has served me much better. I started to shape my new self and life with purpose. Instead of referring to myself as broken, I envisioned what I could be and took steps to shape that.

I started to see the void that needs to be filled in helping women walk through a divorce with eyes on the future. It took me years to course correct my path. I was beginning to recognize that I had choices greater than who the kids spent Christmas with or whether I could live on my income.

My decisions, which the drama and process had so colored, started to be focused on becoming whole.

My victim mentality didn't serve me or anyone I loved. So I started doing the work. And I found help.

Working with a brilliant friend and Holistic Nutrition Coach, Nancy Zitlin, I started to put my body and spirit back together as she supported me through that roller coaster year. I found a business coach, Robyn Crane, who helped me realize it wasn't the career I loathed. I didn't need to "break up" with my job; I learned to seek out a space that would back my vision of helping people balance the financial decisions of divorce with the emotional decisions accompanying it. To build my practice serving instead of selling.

YOUR FIRST STEP

The first step in a divorce is to get ahead of the process and do some work figuring out what you want your life to look like *after*. There will be an after. One of the biggest mistakes made in divorce and perpetuated by the court system? Treating the day your divorce is final as though it's a finish line. Oh, my dear, it's not the end. It is just the beginning.

What does this have to do with the divorce process?

Everything. Going through a divorce isn't linear, and it can imitate cycles of grief in other losses like death. As you progress, your vision may change and become more apparent. Like me, you may experience things that shift your perspective and cause you to course correct.

It is common for goals to change as we progress in our journey. What is important is that we are authentic with ourselves and make sure that our goals still reflect who we are and what we want for our lives. Keep visioning and keep striving toward your best life! You can do this!

This is your one life, and you have a lot more hanging in the balance than anyone involved. Anyone. Even your spouse and children. They are vital, but you cannot control their feelings and opinions. You can't live their lives for them. You can't read their minds. Your children will grow up and lead their own lives. Possibly part of your responsibility in parenting them is to model how they can live their lives well even when dealing with challenging, life-changing events. Even when those are hard things that none of you like.

CHAPTER 1 | DO THE WORK

Vision Board

This is a version of a vision board I created to use in financial workshops. The idea is to arrange your essential things on a time and expense grid. I first ran into the vision board used in this fashion in the book *Picture Your Prosperity* by Ellen Rogin and Lisa Kueng. You can download and print the one I use as a base or create your own. What does it tell you? What is meaningful, and what isn't?

One of the first weekends after my ex-husband moved out and took the kitchen table with him, I got out my old easel, a piece of poster board left over from one kid presentation or another, and a bunch of magazines. Armed with scissors and glue, I set about creating a vision for my future. My good friend Susie stopped by to check on me and found me patching together what I wanted life to look like. I thought it was interesting that she said she hoped she saw me doing something like that. It was a small step to start building a future I could own and believe in. The photos I cut out reminded me of myself and life after the crazy and unknown. I kept that board for years; there were a lot of days it gave me hope and purpose.

Download your vision board template here:

https://bridgingdivorcesolutions.com/vision-board/

Journal

More and more of us journal and consider using it in a directed, focused, and positive way. I suggest using a separate journal that makes you happy when you see it (if you get joy from such things). Write about your dreams and what you may have set aside over time that you can bring back into your life, and take a critical look at how you're living and the parts that are or are not necessary to you.

In that first year after my husband left, I would journal in hope and despair. The sad part just to get it out of my head and put it somewhere else. The jottings ended up in a brown paper grocery bag, one tossed on top of another as the pile grew. As I wrote them and then threw them out, it helped me make space for developing a vision of what could be. Specifically, what could be better?

When journaling here, avoid listing things you don't want or don't like. This is a vision versus a dump. There's a place for dumping; mine was a bunch of written-on scraps in a brown paper bag.

What's your vision? Are there things you've wished you could do but didn't feel that was an option? Possibly your vision is as simple as not falling in the toilet night after night when you get up to go to the bathroom. Perhaps it's ordering exactly what you want on a pizza, no cheese, and extra mushrooms; why not? Or changing careers. Travel? Running a marathon or getting certified in yoga?

All those years ago, when I hated my job and was on the verge of a breakdown as my marriage broke down, I started envisioning a career where I could help people and feel good about it daily. I visioned a relationship that was healthy and joyful. I imagined finding my creativity again after burying it for so long. I even imagined not living in fear of making a wrong move. I fearlessly make mistakes all the time now.

What's your vision?

Letter to your future self

This is surprisingly powerful. Imagine yourself in five years. Where are you living, working, and traveling? Who is in your life, and what does your day look like? Write a letter to your future self as though everything you dream of has happened. Use active words, "I am," and avoid future tense, like "I will."

I did this in year one and opened it in year three. I was shocked to read that everything I'd written about, in great detail, to future Brenda had happened. And faster than five years. And some of them weren't the things I wanted anymore. Don't be afraid to course correct. I continue to rewrite my story. You get to rewrite yours.

Sticky Note Party

I love post-its. I've used them to study, plan, and organize. You can use them to help clarify what is and isn't essential to you.

Get yourself a bunch of post-it notes and something you like to write with. Do a complete dump of everything you can think of

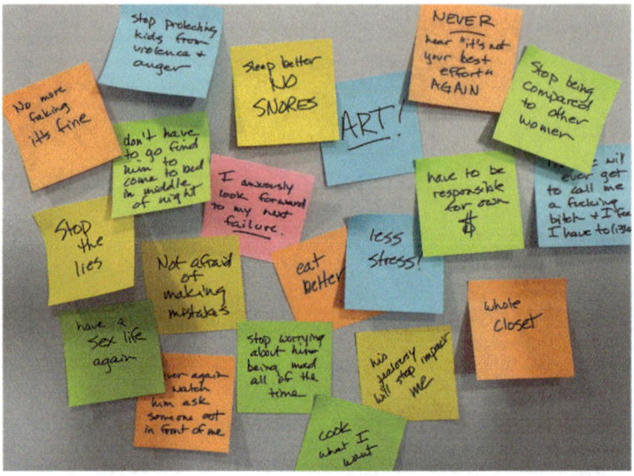

that's an outcome of the divorce. It doesn't matter how big or small. What's keeping you up at night? What do you find exciting? Keep writing and writing and writing until you can't think of anything else, sticking them on the wall as you go. Don't censor yourself as you put this together. It can be as small as who will mow the lawn or as big as I've always hated this house, and now I will be stuck in it.

Once you can't think of anything else to write, start sorting them out. Here are some categories you can use:

- Temporary: These are things happening right now that will fall away down the road. An example of this might be that you think your soon-to-be ex is spending far too much money on dining out now that you are not making meals.
- Immediately post-divorce: These may require a lifestyle or standard of living change. Examples might be thrift shopping instead of department stores or a cute BYOB instead of a high-end steak joint.
- Long-term impact: This includes things that can shape your life and/or something you cannot quickly recover from. An example might be spending the money saved for your children's college on the professional fees for your divorce.

In each category, decide how your notes rank and arrange them to represent how you feel right now.

CHAPTER 1 | RESULT

One turning point in the divorce process was when I realized that I needed to focus on becoming whole again rather than dwelling on my victim mentality. What's your focus?

Write your vision statement here:

This is your life. You decide your process and goals. THEN you match everything else to it.

CHAPTER 1 | **HIGHLIGHTS**

The single most common comment heard from my clients is that they don't know where to start.

- The first step is to think beyond the end of the marriage and clarify what you want your life to look like post-divorce.
- Hiring an attorney may be the right choice for some, but it's not always the first step.
- It is important to be mindful of what you want and how it can impact your future before making any decisions.
- Having goals and a vision for your future can help you stay on track during challenging times.
- Radical acceptance was one mantra that helped turn things around for the author.

CHAPTER 2

Dignity and Grace: A Long Thought Share

The art of life lies in a constant readjustment to our surroundings.
—Kakuzo Okakura

DIGNITY AND GRACE. My mantra and true north.

When I first embraced the words dignity and grace, I really meant I was going to checklist the #$&* out of doing divorce right. I am going to be Teflon. No one will see me cry. No one will see me waiver. I will be fucking fine. No, FINE.

That's not dignity. That's perfectionism.

My new definition of dignity is walking through this world unashamed of my actions. Being true to myself and not trying to mold myself into a different person to make others happy. Being willing to stay strong in my convictions and not having the need to try to convince anyone else of them.

I've moved dramatically from no one will see me cry to crying all the time. I weep when I think of my pup, who died last fall. I cry with pride when I think of my children. I cry when I stand up in a room full of financial advisors and expose my vulnerability. I melt when I see that there can be such beauty in simple things. I cry in gratitude, and still, I sob in grief. I'm writing this as I just returned from my Dad's birthday celebration, which will probably be his last.

Instead of finding dignity in making everything look as shiny and perfect, and unrealistic as possible, I find dignity in experiencing everything I can in the most authentic way I am able.

I think dignity is only being around people I choose to be around. That's not shameful. In my book, it's simply admitting that I am not for everyone and that everyone is not for me.

I find dignity in the single-mindedness of my daughter in pursuing her dreams. I find dignity in my son's vulnerability, realizing he may not want to be a surgeon after all in his third year of medical school and being open to see what comes next. I find dignity and even more grace in my middle child's openness to building a future relationship with me after I messed up so many things and made so many mistakes during and after my divorce.

Divorce can completely disassemble all you've known and worked toward. It can put you in places you never wanted to visit and make you set up camp. It can create crazy from calm and havoc from order.

There will be not-so-good decisions, there will be judgment, and there will be bad days. But they will pass because we're all human, and nobody is perfect.

My hope is for your dignity.

Figure out who you want to be when this is over, and be that person now, not perfectly, to the best of your ability. Stay in touch with what you want. How do you want your life to unfold? Stay aligned with that vision and increase the chances of hanging on to your dignity. And if you lose sight of it for a while as I did, it's never too late to recenter. And to forgive yourself. There's the grace.

As you've no doubt guessed, most of this book is intended to give you the tools that will allow you to stay on track and not go off the rails. If you do, notice it and try to figure out why. Was there something that triggered you? Is there something you can do, for yourself, to stop that from happening?

Do the work. Allow for vulnerability and your own humanity. Figure out what you want and adjust, one step at a time.

This balancing act may be the biggest one you will ever face. You are balancing financial, fact-based decisions with emotions. You're dealing with grief as you're supposed to plan for the future. You're taking care of others when you also need to take the best care of yourself.

The subtitle of the book is Guide to Keeping Your Dignity and Dollars. It's not about getting more in your divorce. It's about not spending stupidly because the process will lead you to do that. You can be mindful and make wise money decisions. You can be in touch with the emotional roller coaster you're on, stand up for yourself, and have boundaries.

You can create the process you want on *your* side.

You cannot control what your spouse does. If you're married to someone who buys into the "knock down, drag out, winner takes all" version of divorce that our system promotes and glorifies, you can't change that.

You can tend to your own self and your own actions.

Sometimes divorce gets nasty, and as much as you'd like to take the high road, you're experiencing some very real lows. You can take more drastic steps if you are pulled off course by the behavior you can't control. They're designed to give you time to get back on track and disengage from being caught in a riptide of messed-up divorce madness.

WHAT HAPPENS WHEN DIGNITY AND GRACE LEAVE THE BUILDING?

All you can do is try your best and recognize that the only person you can control is you, and no one else is the boss of you.

I've had clients who are hell-bent on destroying their spouse, even when it is pointed out that their financial demise means they won't be able to provide child or spousal support. They were so hurt they just didn't care.

They were controlling their own actions and taking power over their decisions.

I've worked with clients who agreed to much less than they would have gotten in court because they were worn down by the process and the vindictiveness of their going-to-be ex and just wanted to be done and start anew.

They were also controlling their actions and taking power over their decisions.

Good enough is sometimes just that.

I was mediating a case between a couple who had not been married long but did share assets. There was no question they were going to divorce, but each had different goals.

One spouse wanted to make sure they knew their rights and got their fair share. The other spouse was hurt and angry and wanted to inflict pain on their former partner.

We came to an agreement that didn't satisfy either of them. One ended up paying for more and walking away with less than they thought they deserved. The other found that "winning" the financial round didn't appease their need to make their going-to-be ex feel as much pain as they did.

It was apparent during the discussions the spouse carrying the hurt kept throwing out bigger and bigger numbers to see how far they could push the other, who they saw as the offender. The other kept giving more and more, begrudgingly wanting to be done. When the angry partner accepted their last demand, they had nowhere to go. It was over. They were done. And the hurt was still there. And while the one we'll call the Paying Partner agreed, they weren't happy because they expected to be forgiven. They hoped that agreeing to all the demands would relieve them of the weight of their spouses' anger.

It wasn't the smoothest of processes; sometimes, divorce is agonizingly hard. On the good side, they can move on instead of spending the following year in court and more in legal fees than the dollars at stake during their discussions.

They never identified what they wanted, and it was masked as an argument about money. The "wronged" spouse wanted acknowledgment that they had been wronged, and the "guilty" spouse wanted forgiveness for their betrayal.

Seeing this play out repeatedly is one of the reasons I would love for people going through divorce to make the connection between the impact emotions have on their financial decisions and how their financial choices mess with their feelings.

We are trying to balance how divorce is done in our society. Divorce can take what was a loving bond that is no longer and throw it into the legal system like a business contract to dissolve.

When my daughter was younger, we would take a road trip from Chicago to Tennessee to visit my parents. Along the way, there was a place where you could stand on the state line between Kentucky and Tennessee. She would jump back and forth and shout, "I'm in Kentucky! I'm in Tennessee!" over and over again.

You are jumping back and forth between two states—the one that means you need to be buttoned up and make logical decisions and the one dealing with moving forward from your marriage, one of the most emotional commitments one can make.

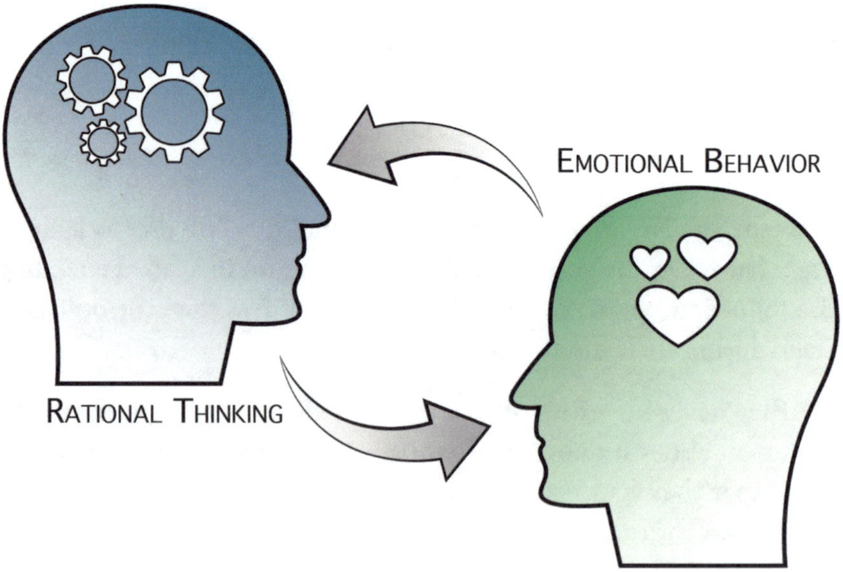

It's confusing.

Allow yourself the grace to realize that.

Looking back, one of my more significant missteps was not revisiting how my situation had shifted over time. When I felt the dynamic of our Collaborative Process meetings change from goal-based to winning-based, and rather than take a step back, understand what that meant, and shift my thinking, I went into a complete panic.

Try not to panic; instead, plan.

I am about a thousand worlds away from my comfort zone writing this. It's far from my standard operating procedure of shining it up, keeping it private, and saying ***everything is fine***.

If one of you reading this course corrects your divorce to better serve you and your family, my discomfort is more than worthwhile.

CHAPTER 2 | DO THE WORK

Journal on the following:

- What do dignity and grace mean to you? Is it important? If not—what is?
- Do you see the interconnect between emotions and finances?
- How can you check in with yourself to see if you are veering off the path?

CHAPTER 2 | RESULT

> Can you find the space to allow for mistakes and give yourself grace? Where does dignity belong in your process?

- You will have a more realistic expectation of the process of divorce, not perfection and not an out-of-control circus.
- You will be grounded in whatever is most important to you—mine was dignity and grace. Define yours.

CHAPTER 2 | **HIGHLIGHTS**

- The divorce process doesn't lend itself to figuring out goals and acknowledging the emotions that affect those goals simultaneously.
- Figuring out what you want as you go through the process, not just money but the emotions and needs behind it, leads to a better resolution.
- Allowing yourself grace if you go off course is good.
- Getting back on course and aligned emotionally and logically is better.

CHAPTER 3

Choosing the Method Right for You

It's not the load that breaks you down,
it's the way you carry it.
—Lena Horne

THE PROCESS YOU PICK DRIVES EVERYTHING. Certainly during and, in many ways, after your divorce is finished.

> Learning about your options and considering how those choices match your situation can save you A LOT of time and money.

Couples often don't know they have choices outside of engaging a lawyer, taking sides, and going to court. Know your options so you can select the method that best suits your situation, your family, and your budget.

Remember, you can *always* become more aggressive in the divorce process. It's difficult to put the genie back in the bottle if you start aggressively and then try to ease into something more amicable.

Lisa found out her husband had lost all their savings through bad investments. He even signed away their home by remortgaging it without her knowledge. She had signed the papers but didn't examine what she was signing. Bill had always managed the finances, and she trusted him to do that. She was busy taking care of the family and running the house. She found out just how bad their financial state was when things were so dire that there was no redeeming their financial situation or marriage. They weren't angry at this point. They were both miserable and frustrated; her husband was extremely ashamed and contrite over his actions. He promised he'd take care of it.

Knowing they were going to divorce, Lisa hired an attorney. This is where things took a turn for the worse. They could have gotten out from under the enormous debt her husband Bill had incurred if they filed for bankruptcy, but he wasn't willing to do that. He thought it would stop him from rebuilding his business in the future. However, he volunteered to take on all the debt he caused. Lisa would walk away without any savings, assets, or support, but she wouldn't be responsible for over half a million dollars that were considered her marital portion.

Instead of listening to their situation and helping them come to a quick and inexpensive agreement, the attorney Lisa hired advised her that if she didn't take an aggressive stance toward Bill, Lisa would have to pay fifty percent of the debt. Since Lisa had "lawyered up," Bill hired his own attorney, who advised him he could get out from under half of the debt by assigning it to Lisa as her marital obligation. It didn't matter that she didn't know about it or have anything to do with it.

This went quickly from a sad while respectful parting of ways to an all-out battle over who would pay the debt. Their process was no longer their own. The attorneys were driving all the choices, timing, and expense. Their attorney fees grew by tens of thousands of dollars, and three years later, they were still not divorced or moving on with their lives. They were no longer speaking, and their four children had taken sides. Their case no longer had much to do with them or the best interests of their family overall.

Most, if not all, of this could have been avoided if Lisa's original advice was to use a mediator and a legal document preparer to draw up their agreement for Bill to take on the debt. Or had Lisa been empowered to take control of the situation, making her own decisions and using her lawyer for guidance instead of letting her run the show.

Don't end up like Lisa and Bill. Honestly, they might have ended up fighting in court anyway. They will never know because they didn't give a less expensive and less aggressive process a chance. Now their family and finances have even more healing to do if they can get past the trauma and expense the divorce caused.

YOU HAVE THE POWER TO CHOOSE!

One style might be better suited to your family and situation. Knowing what kind of divorce you'd like to pursue is the first step and will drive the rest of your decisions, like what professionals you need on your team. (We talk about how to pick your attorney, coaches, or financial specialists in Chapter 14. I suggest you read that before interviewing and hiring potential partners.)

There are four main styles of divorce:

1. Kitchen Table (Pro Se or DIY)

2. Mediation

3. Collaborative Divorce Process

4. Divorce Litigation

These are listed and explained from the least expensive and most cooperative to the most costly and adversarial.

KITCHEN TABLE (PRO SE OR DIY)

Pro Se is the legal phrase for a person who represents themselves. If you or your spouse go this route, you're expected by the court to have the same knowledge as a lawyer while you are representing yourself. You are expected to follow the court procedures, know how to handle yourself in the courtroom, and in essence, know the law.

What does that mean?

It means that if mistakes are made, or you weren't aware of something, you can't come back later and claim ignorance. "I didn't know" isn't a reason to fix something legally wrong with your agreement.

The benefits of representing yourself probably don't outweigh the risks. The advantage is that there are no attorney fees. The dangers or disadvantages are considerable.

Even though a person may think their divorce is "simple," a divorce case is rarely straightforward. When representing yourself, you are also responsible for calculating child support and maintenance (also known as alimony or spousal support), understanding how assets are distributed and making sure that you can actually do what you agree on, dividing retirement accounts (which may not be divisible), and understanding the divorce tax consequences.

Kitchen Table or DIY is another form of self-representation. This differs slightly from Pro Se, where one party is representing themselves and may present in court. Here, the couple determines their settlement and files their forms. Coming up with your own agreement without knowing the rules where you live can be tricky. More complicated situations like dissolving a long-term marriage, couples with minor children, and those with significant joint assets will likely benefit from the guidance of professionals who understand the impact of finances and legal options.

This might be appropriate for those with a short-term marriage and no children or shared assets.

Julie and Carl had been married twenty-seven years, had three grown children, and both worked outside the home. They had comparable incomes and similar retirement savings.

Most importantly, they agreed they didn't want to be married anymore. Neither was looking for or expecting any kind of support from the other.

They came to me looking to move forward with the process correctly and avoid going to court or hiring attorneys. The pair also wanted to make sure what they thought they wanted to do, what had been decided between them, would be a reasonable way to split their finances, and they didn't have any problems they may not have thought about.

After looking at their proposed agreement, I found some issues that would cause Carl to pay thousands of dollars in taxes they weren't aware of. We rearranged how they divided things to share the tax expense evenly, draft their agreement, and work with a settlement-minded attorney to complete the legal part of their filing.

This wasn't entirely a Kitchen Table divorce, but it shows how it's possible to come up with a solid solution with minimum time and expense when the process fits the situation. If Julie and Carl had each retained counsel and filed for divorce first, their costs would have easily been thousands more than they spent.

MEDIATION

Think of Mediation as the process of the couple making their own decisions but having someone to help them if they get stuck. Mediators are trained to assist people in resolving their differences but do not tell them what to do or share their opinions with the couple.

A mediator is a neutral party—they don't take sides. A couple will use one mediator between them; they are not each represented by an individual mediator. When this happens, the person is no longer neutral; they act more like an advisor or coach.

It's important to realize that the mediator does not advise or direct you on what to decide. They are there to help you come to your own decisions.

You may use more than one mediator if that professional has specific expertise. I've mediated the financial portion of a divorce settlement when another professional is helping them through the parenting decisions. This may be useful if the couple needs education or information that a specialist can bring. They still want to make their own decisions and need more options to base those decisions on.

The mediator may be an attorney, a financial professional, or someone in the mental health field, like a therapist or social worker. It's important to realize that the mediator does not advise or direct you on what to decide. They are there to help you come to your own decisions.

How Does Mediation Work?

Mediation is a structured, consensual process that offers divorcing couples an alternative to traditional litigation. All mediators work to help parties settle a dispute using different styles and approaches. Just as physicians or therapists use various techniques to achieve desired results, mediators also use other methods.

The three main ways of mediation that we'll go over are Evaluative, Facilitative, and Transformative. In choosing your mediator, ask them about what style of mediation they practice. If you are expecting Transformative mediation, where you sit down at the same table and work through your agreement, but you have a practitioner who uses Evaluative mediation, where you and your spouse are in separate rooms evaluating offers on the spot, you may be starting out on the wrong foot from the beginning.

Knowing the type of mediation that is used in your area or being able to seek out the type you would like to use can make a world of difference in your outcome.

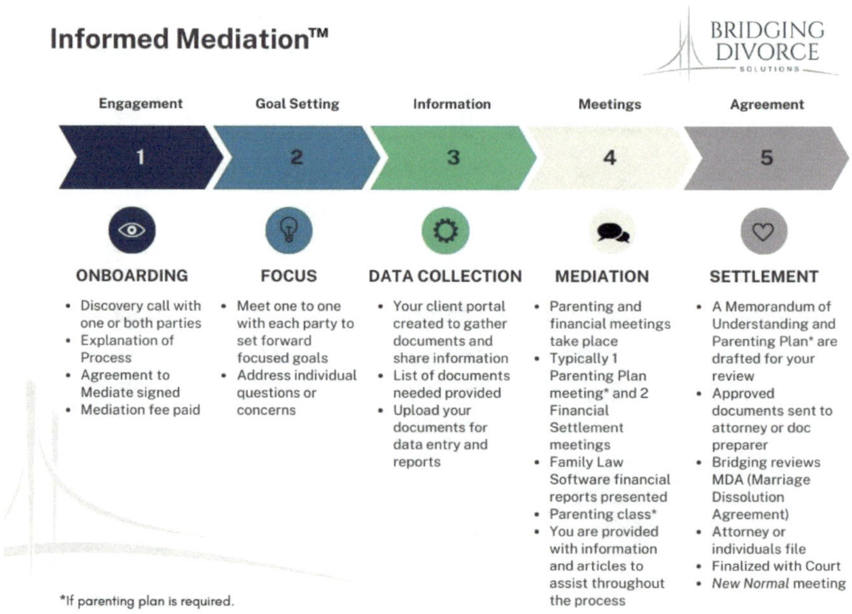

This is the typical flow I use when mediating divorce with my clients; other mediators may have a different process.[7]

7 Mediation Plus® is used with permission of and credit to Smarter Divorce Solutions.

What Are the Types of Mediation in Family Law?

Following sums up different styles, there are three. One style may suit your needs better than another. Ask your mediator what their style is so you know if it's a match.

1) Evaluative Mediation

This can be a no-nonsense style based on negotiation; it's typically a business-oriented practice. Evaluative mediators work quickly and efficiently to get to the point and draft a solution. They are more likely to give opinions and make recommendations based on their experience. In this case, they are not always a neutral party and may actually either appear to take a side or actually take a side. Think of this as someone who wants to "cut to the chase" and get finished.

Evaluative mediation can be extremely useful when there are time pressures to come to a decision and if the problem being mediated is relatively factual. An evaluative mediation may make a lot of sense with a subject like how to assign a value to a business based on the revenue and balance sheets for the past several years.

Evaluative mediation is the most likely to have the professional give their point of view or advice, to provide facts or information, and guide the decisions being made.

2) Transformative Mediation

A transformative approach provides time and space for the parties to listen and understand one another. Transformative mediators are likely to create room for emotions to be communicated through the process and to allow emotional healing with the solution. It is common in a transformative mediation that the parties involved gain new insight as to the point of view and position of the other. This can help them more easily examine a situation from multiple sides instead of taking a solid position.

Transformative mediators are especially useful when conflicts are more intensely personal and when parties desire empowerment and recognition. Think of this as getting to the problem underlying what is being discussed. Sometimes just the recognition that people have different points of view can help people come to a solution that meets, or at least addresses, the needs of both parties.

Transformative mediation is more likely to allow the couple to decide what they will or won't address and come up with their own answers based on the information they bring to the table. The mediator here will help handle emotions but is less likely to bring information or options to the process.

3) Facilitative Mediation

In between these two styles of mediation are facilitative mediators. This style of mediation could be the most familiar. Facilitative mediators tend to adapt to the parties' needs as they work through the decisions they need to make. They may use approaches from both evaluative and transformative practices.

In facilitative mediation, the professional helps to provide a constructive environment for couples to work together and make decisions around essential issues such as the division of assets and debts, custody arrangements, support payments, and other matters related to their divorce. A professional mediator will guide the parties through the process by facilitating communication, ensuring that all discussion takes place in a respectful manner, and presenting options so that both parties can come to an agreement that works for them. This approach typically results in cost savings as well as improved relationships between former partners. Facilitative mediation provides divorcing couples with an effective way of resolving disputes without lengthy court proceedings.

Using a facilitative style, a mediator asks questions, normalizes viewpoints, and validates each person's points of view. Facilitative mediators provide a balance of evaluative and transformative styles.

Here's an example of what can happen when the style of mediation you expect isn't what you actually experience.

Jennifer and her husband were required to participate in court-ordered mediation before the case advanced in the judicial system. Jennifer, who had not worked outside of the home for seventeen years, was trying to be as thoughtful and considerate as possible during the process. She had spent a lot of time working through her budget and earning potential, figuring out what she thought would be best for their children and coming up with a settlement outline that would allow her to get back on her feet and be affordable for her husband. She didn't think it was greedy or outlandish and had a solid rationale for each point of her proposal. She knew what she thought was ideal, but she also realized that Tad, her husband, would have his own goals. Jennifer also knew what the bare minimum was she could get by on, so she went into her mediation hoping that they could come to an agreement and move on.

What Jennifer didn't know was that the mediation style she would encounter was not based on goals or discussion. The mediator traveled between rooms; one room for

Jennifer and her attorney and the other for her spouse and his attorney. Their mediator started with her husband. About half an hour later, he came into the room where Jennifer sat waiting and tossed a piece of paper on the table with the "offer." There was no context to the numbers or rationale behind where they started. Jennifer tried to discuss what she had worked on with her attorney so that they could explain why she was asking for the support and assets she thought were equitable. Because their mediator didn't practice this style, and both attorneys really just wanted to see what the other side was proposing so they could use it in litigation, Jennifer and Tad's mediation failed before it even got started. Jennifer's attorney told her that her goals had nothing to do with mediation.

Is Mediation Right for You?

Divorce mediation is an effective option for couples seeking to divorce in a respectful, efficient manner. Mediation might be the process you choose if you are willing to work together and communicate openly in order to reach an agreement on matters such as the division of assets and debts, custody arrangements, support payments, and other issues related to your divorce.

You can have mediation as part of the litigation process; many states in an effort to have more of the family law decisions made outside of the courtroom, require a couple to try to reach an agreement through mediation before they pursue a divorce case in the court system. This is not a freestanding mediation process; it can be inserted into litigation.

If you choose mediation to come to a settlement agreement outside of the courtroom, you need to be in a position where you trust each other enough to believe that there are not any hidden agendas or facts. If someone is having relationships outside of the marriage or hiding money or otherwise not being fully truthful, mediation is probably not the best solution for you because you may not be making decisions based on full disclosure of the facts or finances.

When couples can agree to be forthcoming with information and open in discussions, mediation can help reduce both the emotional toll and financial expense that can come with traditional court proceedings. The mediation process provides a safe space for both parties to express their feelings and opinions without feeling judged or pressured. It's carried out in private at the pace the couple chooses. Because of its cost-effectiveness and efficiency, divorce mediation is often more beneficial than litigation and provides many individuals with the closure they need. With mediation, your goal is not to stay together but rather to separate your lives with as much consensus and as little fighting and expense as possible.

COLLABORATIVE DIVORCE

> When two people decide to get a divorce,
> it isn't a sign that they 'don't understand' one another,
> but a sign that they have, at least, begun to.
> —Helen Rowland

Collaborative Divorce is a legal process becoming more popular, and well known, as families try to make better decisions around divorce that cost less in emotional and financial capital. It started in the 1990s when a family law attorney, Stu Webb, recognized the damage caused by the court system in divorce and envisioned what he believed was a better way for families to reshape themselves and control their own decisions.

The Collaborative Process uses Alternative Dispute Resolution and all the decisions are made by the couple outside of the courtroom. The Collaborative Process allows couples to negotiate all the terms of a divorce based on the goals they establish at the beginning of their process. You and your spouse use a combination of assisted mediation and negotiation to agree on the essential terms of the divorce, like property and debt division, child custody and child support, and spousal support. These decisions are made with the guidance of attorneys, but the conversations are between the divorcing couple, not their legal counsel.

Your state may or may not have formal laws supporting the Collaborative Process. If you reside in a state that hasn't formally recognized Collaborative Divorce in their family law system, you may still be able to find attorneys, Certified Divorce Coaches® and Certified Divorce Financial Analysts® who are familiar with the practice and can support you in a hybrid of the system that allows you to make your decisions privately with the support of trained professionals.

How Does Collaborative Divorce Work?

The Collaborative Divorce Process begins with a commitment between spouses to negotiate and work together in this goals-based approach. A collaborative divorce won't work if either party is unwilling to participate or be truthful. This doesn't mean you need to be on great terms. You can solve hard things around the Collaborative table with the proper support from professionals who are used to the practice.

After choosing Collaborative Process, the first step is for you and your spouse to hire professionals trained in the Collaborative Divorce Practice. Your team includes an attorney for each party, a financial neutral, and one or two divorce coaches. Depending on your needs, other professionals, like child specialists or a mediator, may become involved.

A caution. If a professional says, "sure, I can do that," but hasn't been trained in the process of Alternative Dispute Resolution on which Collaborative Practice is based, proceed with extreme caution. I've seen well-intentioned practitioners go off-track if not trained because they revert to a more traditional litigation approach. One sign that your professional team is going off-track is when the "let's make a deal" approach is used during the process to direct clients as though they were bargaining in litigation.

Joseph and Elaine wanted to use the Collaborative practice to figure out their settlement and the custody arrangement for their two sons. Their situation was more complicated than most because Joseph owned his own business, and Elaine, as an executive, had a compensation package that included Restricted Stock Options and substantial performance bonuses. They also owned two houses, one of which was co-owned by Elaine's parents, who lived there. Before learning about the Collaborative process, Joseph hired an attorney who practiced traditional litigation. His attorney was known to be a "bulldog" who loved to go to court.

Elaine learned about the Collaborative practice at a workshop she attended and shared the information about the process with Joseph. He agreed that deciding on an agreement privately with the benefit of attorneys, a Divorce Coach, and a CDFA® was much more compelling than years of battling it out in court. He'd already hired an attorney and paid a nonrefundable retainer, so he asked his attorney if he could represent him in the Collaborative Process. His attorney agreed, and they started their team meetings.

Joseph and Elaine, as well as the remainder of the team, became more and more frustrated. As they would agree on a particular subject, Joseph's attorney would regularly throw a wrench in the process, and he kept asking for more. He was so entrenched in the legal negotiation mindset he was used to practicing that he couldn't allow Elaine and Joseph to make decisions they were comfortable with. It was as if when they decided something, Joseph's attorney saw the opportunity to "win" more and swooped in to ask for it.

After several meetings where agreements were reached and then unraveled, Elaine decided to leave the process and hire a litigator who would take over dealing with Joseph's confrontational attorney. This is the only Collaborative Process I've been involved with that failed to reach a conclusion. I strongly believe it was because the entire team of professionals involved wasn't well versed in the process being "goal-based" instead of "winning-based." I lost touch with the parties' status after three years, but at that time, they were still in court. Fighting.

Experienced Collaborative Divorce professionals are well-versed in supporting a goals-based, win-win settlement for both parties. A significant difference between Collaborative Process and mediation is the involvement of individual attorneys during the meetings in support of their clients. In this process, lawyers represent each party's interests. That means if you aren't comfortable with or sure about the terms of your divorce, your attorney is there to clarify and advocate for you.

Another benefit of the Collaborative Process is conversations are held in real-time with all present, so the likelihood of things being "lost in translation" is much smaller. You also have specialists working with you and your spouse in their areas of expertise. Having a financial specialist supporting the financial decisions and a mental health professional or coach supporting family decisions can significantly lower the chance of mistakes and increase the agreement's durability. Meaning? You are less likely to end up in court down the road.

In Collaborative Divorce, you manage the process and the schedule. At the beginning of the process, you typically sign a Participation Agreement stating your intent is to use the process and make your decisions privately, not in a public courtroom. The gravity of this agreement holds each party accountable and is a strong incentive for the spouses to negotiate, even when the conversations get complicated.

You each voluntarily provide any information necessary to continue negotiations, such as tax returns, employment and salary information, and all other information regarding assets and debts. There is no divorce discovery in Collaborative Divorce; you have to trust that your spouse has provided all relevant information. If you are concerned your spouse will hide information from you, then Collaborative Divorce may not be your best option.

This is the process my team follows for a Collaborative Divorce:

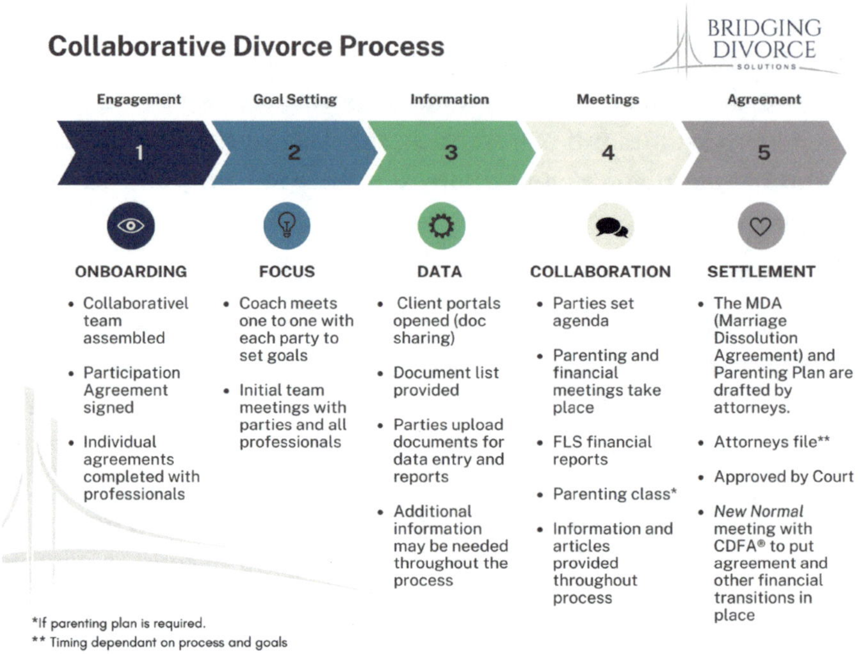

Is Collaborative Divorce Right for You?

Each of you must be willing to negotiate a goals-based agreement to accomplish your Collaborative Divorce. You also have to be open to working together and meeting face-to-face (even if that face-to-face is on Zoom). If you and your spouse have a history of abuse or a power imbalance, the likelihood of the process working for you is reduced.

If you are willing to set aside your differences and talk rationally, you may save time and money and reduce hostility using the Collaborative Process.

The Collaborative Divorce Process can be highly effective for those transitioning from long-term marriages with more complicated financial structures and children involved. It's also favored by people who want to keep their divorce discussions private instead of playing them out in a courtroom or having them be part of a public record someone can look up in the future.

One thing you should be aware of before starting the Collaborative Process is that the Participation Agreement requires that if you or your spouse decide to leave the process at any time, you both must start with a new team of professionals. Your attorney in a Collaborative Divorce is also precluded from taking your case over to litigation if the process isn't successful. This, in part, is to nullify the threat of "I'm just going to take you to court" if discussions are not going the way one party thought they would.

Collaborative Process may be right for you if you like the idea of making your own decisions privately and still want the advice of attorneys as you navigate the often confusing journey of divorce decisions. If you have concerns about legal aspects of your decisions, having attorneys present (unlike solely using a mediator for your process) can provide peace of mind and assurance of a legally sound agreement.

DIVORCE LITIGATION

Litigation is based on the court system, even if the divorcing couple doesn't go to court. When parties choose this method, they rely on attorneys and the legal system to negotiate their agreement, usually based on what the law in their jurisdiction will allow. They ultimately depend on the court to decide the things they can't agree on. On the one hand, if the couple is incapable of making decisions together, this can be a good thing. On the other, it can be a big risk because you're allowing your life and your family's lives to be dictated by someone who doesn't know you, your family, or your situation. If those decisions are being made by a judge, you're also inviting someone who will bring their own view and set of ethics and morals to their decisions. They might be very distant from yours.

A drawback of litigation is that if you are using this process for your divorce, you are participating in, and at the mercy of, an out-of-date and backlogged court system. It's not unusual for a divorce to take a year or two to wind its way through the family court system. Even if you don't start with a great deal of contention at the beginning of the process, the stress and expense of months or years of coming to closure can certainly stir it up.

The litigation process can be mentally and emotionally exhausting, and budgets can be difficult to control. Since litigation is by nature adversarial and public, it also affects other family members, your children, your extended family, and your friends.

How Does Litigation Work?

When you're litigating divorce settlement, you are using attorneys to represent you and your best interests in coming to a settlement agreement. Your spouse is also represented by an attorney, and those two attorneys will negotiate the terms of any division of assets or debt, the support that will be paid by one party to another for a child or to the ex-spouse, and the custodial time a parent spends with their children.

There is no certain path in litigating divorce, and the steps can vary greatly depending on the attorney you hire, the attorney who is representing your spouse, the jurisdiction you live in, and how the courts are structured. All this, as well as, the laws that rule over all the decisions you need to make.

Here is an idea of the process represented visually—remember it's not linear. A tornado may be a better representation.

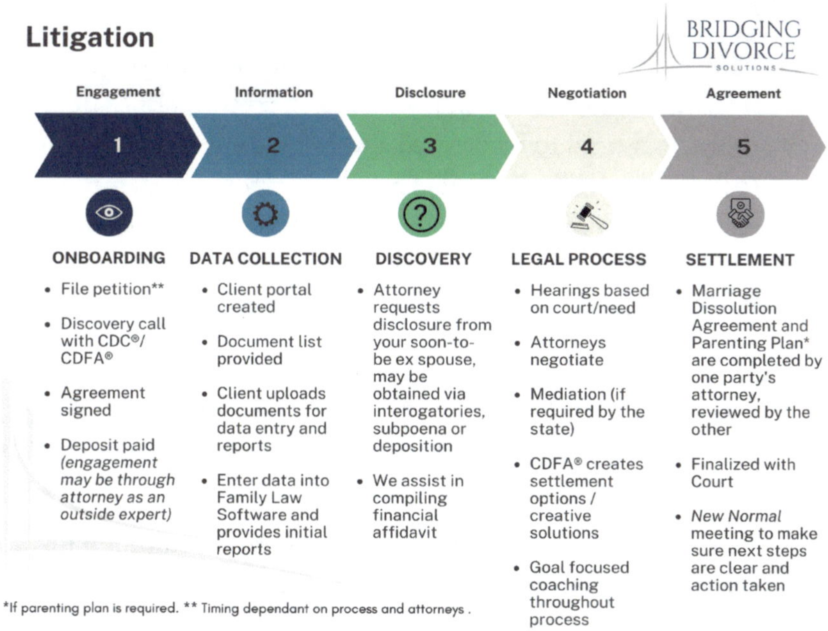

What You May Expect Is:

- Either you or your spouse (or both) will hire an attorney.
- You may file for divorce and have your spouse "served" the papers about the filing.
  - Your spouse, if they are the plaintiff (the one asking for the divorce), may file and have you served with the papers.
- You will meet with your attorney for a preliminary briefing about your case, whether there is a reason for the divorce that will impact the legal proceedings or not, and what your concerns are and their next steps.

- Your attorney and your spouse's attorney may discuss the case to determine the next steps, OR your attorney and your spouse's attorney may resort to using the process of the court system to move your case forward.
- Under the jurisdiction where you live (or the place you are filing if you don't both live there), your attorneys will start to discuss things that need to be decided and bring those to you and your spouse to weigh in on. These may be temporary orders that you and your spouse decide upon while you go through the process, like parenting schedules or how money will be spent, or they may be steps toward coming to a final agreement that will be your permanent settlement.
- If hearings are being scheduled for the court to make decisions on either the permanent or temporary orders, these can happen along the way.
- As you move through the litigation process, it's common for your attorneys to conduct discovery. Discovery is an attorney putting in an official request for information that they want to be provided by the other side. Then the individual is compelled to answer their requests within a given period. Often the answers are not complete, and there's a lot of back-and-forth trying to get the information your attorney has requested, and vice versa.
- During this back-and-forth, your attorney will be assessing the information regarding your case and perhaps consulting with your spouse's attorney to reach an agreement.
    - If your divorce is contentious, this might not be taking place and your attorney may be spending their time building a case against your spouse based on the information they have gathered or continue to seek new information based on where the information they've gotten so far leads them.

- Most litigation cases are settled out of court, but not before going through much of the back-and-forth process between attorneys, hearings, discovery, and court dates. [8] When people come to the realization that a judge might be deciding against them just as much as they might rule in their favor, and usually a case settles by the couple reaching an agreement.
- If your case is heard before a judge, either preliminarily or as a final decision, your attorney and your spouse's attorney will have the opportunity to present whatever evidence they have gathered that is admissible to make a case against you. The judge (and, in some cases, jury) listens to both sides and determines what they think should happen based on their interpretation of the best interests of the family and what is correct under the law. This ruling is final unless you choose to try to appeal it later—resulting in more time and cost.

Is Litigation Right for You?

Litigation might be the right course of action for you if you are involved in a marriage where you and your spouse just can't come to an agreement on things like support and parenting. This may also be best if you are getting divorced for cause (see the box below for common legal causes for divorce). Or you may be in a situation where there is a big imbalance of power and you need an attorney to stand up to an abusive partner.

8 "Divorce Information & Articles | Lawyers.com." n.d. Www.lawyers.com. Accessed March 24, 2023. https://www.lawyers.com/legal-info/family-law/divorce/.

Common Grounds for At-Fault Divorce[8]

1. *Adultery or cheating*
1. *Bigamy*
1. *Desertion*
1. *Mental incapacity at the time of marriage*
1. *Marriage between close relatives*
1. *Impotence at time of marriage*
1. *Force or fraud in obtaining the marriage*
1. *Criminal conviction and/or imprisonment*
1. *Mental or physical abuse*
1. *Drug or alcohol addiction*
1. *Mental illness*

Know that if this is the course of action you choose, you are giving up much of the control over decisions for your divorce, how much the process will cost, and how long it will take. There are plenty of reasons that litigating might be the right course of action. The court system is there to protect the rights of citizens, and they can protect the rights of individuals in divorce as part of this. If one is looking at the courts as a way to have their grievances heard or shame someone, it can very well do so. The courts can also hear your case and decide definitively against your point of view. You are always taking a risk by allowing someone else to make decisions for you.

Litigation can be costly and time-consuming, so it's important to weigh all of your options before deciding whether or not to go to court. If you have any questions about divorce litigation or any other aspect of the divorce process, a qualified family law attorney is your best source for guidance. *Consider Chapter 14, How to Interview Professionals,* to help you find the best match for you.

Remember, going to court is giving a judge permission to make decisions for you even though they may understand little about your family and background. In litigation, you are potentially turning over the decisions about your children, your property, your money, and how you live your life to a third party. And, on the more anecdotal side, you don't know what type of day that judge is having when they hear your case. Did they sleep poorly the night before? Are they upset about their kid's grades? Did they just hear four cases prior to yours that all have a similar fact pattern so you'll get a similar decision?

Lastly, consider that the records of your case are available to the public. This includes your children, your co-workers, and your neighbors. If you're concerned about privacy; this may not be the best option for you.

Forbes reveals the average cost of divorce in 2022 to be $15,000 per person. [9]According to attorneys I've informally interviewed about cost, most say that a couple can't litigate for less than $20,000 per person. When couples can't agree on things like child custody and property settlements, the professional fees can escalate to six figures quickly.[10]

9 Lang, Tyler. 2022. "Council Post: The Financial Impact of Divorce." Forbes. October 20, 2022. https://www.forbes.com/sites/forbesfinancecouncil/2022/10/20/the-financial-impact-of-divorce/.

10 Crail, Chauncey. 2022. "How Much Does a Divorce Cost in 2022? – Forbes Advisor." Www.forbes.com. July 29, 2022. https://www.forbes.com/advisor/legal/divorce/how-much-does-divorce-cost/.

Why the variance? Reporting isn't the same everywhere, and it isn't always sorted the same way; you can have $200,000 in litigated cases and $500 DIY feeding into the statistics.

Some jurisdictions or cases can cost significantly more, even hundreds of thousands of dollars. When disputes over child support, child custody, and alimony occur, decisions take longer, cost more, and tend to become more contentious. The average length of time to litigate divorce is twelve to eighteen months.[11] Even a "simple" uncontested divorce takes about eight months.[12]

WHAT NEXT?

Divorce can be chaotic and scary. Both of you will probably experience extreme emotions while ending your relationship. It's not likely that you both walk away feeling like you received everything you wanted. The more open-minded and future-oriented you are, the more likely you will use a process that suits you and obtain an outcome that supports how you want to reshape your relationship.

11 Michon, Kathleen, and Attorney. n.d. "How Much Will My Divorce Cost and How Long Will It Take?" Www.nolo.com. https://www.nolo.com/legal-encyclopedia/ctp/cost-of-divorce.html.

12 Sember, Brette. 2022. "How Long Does a Divorce Take? – Forbes Advisor." Www.forbes.com. September 28, 2022. https://www.forbes.com/advisor/legal/divorce/how-long-does-divorce-take/.

CHAPTER 3 | DO THE WORK

- Do the **Pick Your Process Workbook**, **Module: Emotional Check-In**

- Read Chapter 14 before you interview professionals

CHAPTER 3 | RESULT

How will I let go of this marriage and embrace a new chapter in my life, even though it may be uncertain and filled with unknowns?

- You'll have a plan to move forward in an educated, informed way.
- You'll know the pros and cons of these decisions at the beginning of the process.
- You'll be more likely to select a process that is the best for you and your family instead of jumping into the legal system if that doesn't serve you.

CHAPTER 3 | **HIGHLIGHTS**

- You have a wide range of options for divorce proceedings.
- Understanding the different processes and choosing the one that best fits your particular situation can save time, money, and a lot of stress.
- Doing research early on and carefully selecting the process that best suits your family will help you all have a smooth and less costly transition into the next stage of life.

CHAPTER 4

Reality Check. Set Yourself Up for Success

It is our attitude at the beginning of a difficult task which, more than anything else, will affect its successful outcome.
—William James

You are more than likely in one of two places at the beginning of the process—-either you are the one looking for a divorce, you've been thinking about it for a long time and you're ready to move forward, or you are not as far along in the process as your spouse. Maybe you were completely taken by surprise when your spouse told you they wanted a divorce. Or maybe you weren't shocked at all because you know things were in a bad place, but you weren't as far down the path as your spouse in accepting divorce.

Either way, a reality check at this point is a good thing. In this chapter, we'll take a look at where you're coming from and some of the important things you need to do to make your divorce, AND your life after divorce, go more smoothly.

ARE YOU AHEAD OF YOUR SPOUSE? GIVE THEM TIME.

Now that you've decided to move forward, you may want to rush to the finish line so you can start your new life.

If you're the partner who wants the divorce, you've had more time to process what you want. Maybe you dream about life after marriage; you can already see moving on and what's next for you.

You've probably looked things up online, perhaps read blogs, or attended webinars. Take a second and think about how long you've been processing this decision. How long were you sure before you told your spouse divorce is your choice? Even with all that, you sometimes still might feel unsure or confused. Give them the grace of time to get used to this new reality.

IT'S NORMAL TO FEEL A WIDE RANGE OF EMOTIONS, INCLUDING SADNESS, ANGER, FEAR, AND CONFUSION.

Are you familiar with cognitive dissonance? *Cognitive dissonance* is when you feel really uncomfortable because you have two different ideas or beliefs that don't make sense together. For example, if you know smoking is bad for your health but still smoke, you might feel guilty or stressed because your actions don't match what you believe. People want their thoughts and actions to make sense and match each other, so it can be hard when they don't.

Enter divorce. It's not at all unusual to experience this back and forth over and over again in the process. You want a divorce. You tell your spouse. You're relieved and moving forward. WAIT. Do you want a divorce? You still want to have dinner at home and tuck in the kids. It's possible you even want to snuggle up to your going-to-be ex from time to time.

Or you don't want the divorce, and you're struggling to adapt. But you just got home from a hard day and you weren't expected to make dinner, or do laundry. As you pour a glass of wine and put on Ted Lasso with a takeout order of guacamole and chips, maybe you feel a little bit of ease. WAIT. You don't want a divorce. But, maybe, sometimes you do.

It's real, and it's normal. This isn't a linear experience.

ARE YOU THE LEFT-BEHIND SPOUSE? BE CAREFUL OF WISHFUL THINKING.

The "left-behind" spouse is a term you may come across describing the person in the marriage who was left, the person who didn't want the divorce. If that's you, how you show up in this space can have an enormous amount of impact on where you go from here.

Divorce is never easy, and for the left-behind spouse, it can feel like the end of the world. You may be tempted to hold on to hope that your relationship can be salvaged despite all evidence pointing to the contrary. This wishful thinking can be a dangerous trap, preventing you from moving forward and healing from the pain of divorce.

Wishful thinking keeps you trapped and spinning.

John Maxwell, in his book, *Mentoring 101*, notes, "The greatest achievers in life are people who set goals for themselves and then work hard to reach them. What they get by reaching the goals is not nearly as important as what they become by reaching them."

What does this have to do with divorce? Maxwell is addressing some of the fallout of **neuroplasticity**—the ability of your brain to rewire itself. This doesn't happen by reaching a goal; it happens by taking small steps on a regular basis.

What motivates you about moving forward into your new life? You may need to dig deep, but when you do, you will probably find what it is that keeps you moving forward. And when you do, it should be about you and the life you want to live, the path you want to walk. Make sure to do "The Work" at the end of this chapter to figure out what that is for you.

It's important to accept reality and start making necessary changes for your future. This doesn't mean giving up on love or happiness but rather recognizing that they may come in different forms than you once imagined. Seek support from friends, family, or a therapist who can help you navigate this challenging time with grace and strength. Remember that you are worthy of love and happiness, even if it looks different from what you once thought it would be.

EMPOWER YOURSELF: HOW TO BREAK FREE OF THE VICTIM MINDSET

Often, it's inviting to take on the role of victim. I'll admit that I took this on in my own divorce. After all the years of allowing. Of sacrifice. Of taking care of everything else and everybody else—this? This is what I get? Victim. It was an unfortunate number of years before I was able to move beyond that particular lens and see the role I took in my marriage AND the role I continued to play in my recovery. As you've heard me say before, I don't want that for you.

It's time to face victimhood and move on.

Getting out of this trap is hard until you recognize it. After you start seeing your patterns and where they're helping you or holding you back, you can start to do something about them. Ending your relationship with being a victim in the divorce gives you your power back. This, probably more than anything else, will help you make good decisions in the process and afterward. When you give up the cozy cloak of victimhood, you stop being the person to whom something was done. You start owning your life, your present. If you have children, you're a better model for them. And then you can actually start building your own new reality and work on creating a life you love, bit by bit. A life that gives you the gift of authenticity and lets you walk away from bitterness and ugliness. Who wants to live there?

DIVORCE CAN BE A LONG AND DIFFICULT PROCESS THAT REQUIRES PATIENCE AND RESILIENCE.

One of my main reasons for writing this is to make divorce less damaging, less expensive, and less time-consuming. Be ready for the reality that it may cost more, take longer, and do more damage than you want.

Being mindful of this can help minimize it. Also, know it's not a process you can be in control of unless you and your spouse (and the court if that's the route you're taking) are 100 percent on the same page.

THE LEGAL SYSTEM MAY NOT FEEL LIKE IT'S ON YOUR SIDE OR WORKING IN YOUR BEST INTEREST.

Family law courts are working within the rules of your state, overburdened time-wise, and can never have the complete experience of your family. Having an expectation they will see your facts (and stories) the same way you do is setting yourself up for disappointment. Even if your attorney or judge understands the basis of your story, the laws where you live may not be on your "side."

SELF-CARE IS CRUCIAL AS YOU RIDE THE EMOTIONAL ROLLERCOASTER OF DIVORCE.

Self-care takes many forms. What works for one person may not work for another. Some people find that exercise or meditation helps manage stress levels, while others might prefer spending time with friends or finding a new hobby. Search for activities that bring you peace and help you feel more grounded.

In divorce, you're dealing with uncertainty that comes with major life changes. Taking care of yourself can help you build resilience and cope with these changes in a healthier way. When you prioritize your own needs, you're better equipped to handle whatever else comes your way.

Remember: self-care isn't selfish—it's essential. Taking care of yourself sets you up for a brighter, healthier future.

It's important to remember that these are just some common realities of divorce, and everyone's experience differs depending on circumstances. Seeking support from loved ones or professionals can help you manage these challenges and come out stronger on the other side.

CHAPTER 4 | DO THE WORK

- What are some areas you may need a reality check? Who can you work with to support that? Are you ready and willing to hear some truths that may be difficult?

CHAPTER 4 | RESULT

Greek chorus: a group of people who, with persistence, express especially similar views or feelings about a particular action or series of actions.

Who do you want to make your decisions? Are you dealing with the "Greek Chorus" or good information that will inform and guide you?

- You are aware of some places you may have blinders on, now and throughout the process.
- If you are experiencing emotions that are clouding your ability to get a good reality check, get support from professionals able to walk through this with you. Specifically, ask them to "reality-check" you, so you are not acting on information that is not solid.

CHAPTER 4 | **HIGHLIGHTS**

Give your spouse time to adjust to the divorce.

- Experiencing a range of emotions and cognitive dissonance is normal during divorce, as it can be difficult for thoughts and actions to align with each other.
- Accepting reality and seeking support is crucial for the left-behind spouse to move forward and heal from divorce.
- Letting go of victimhood in divorce empowers individuals to make better decisions and create a new, authentic reality that is free from bitterness.
- Family law courts have limited time and resources; must act under the laws of your state and may not comprehend the complexities of your unique situation.
- Practicing self-care not only helps with coping and resilience during a divorce, but it can also lead to making better decisions.

CHAPTER 5

Divorce Myths—Let's Call 'Em Out

Myths which are believed in tend to become true.
—George Orwell

NOT A DAY GOES BY in my work with clients that I don't hear some form of divorce myth. Know how to separate fact from fiction, so you're not making your choices based on hearsay that was shared with you while waiting for your grande cappuccino.

Not long ago, I got a call from Jane. She had been living in a marriage she'd considered over for years. She was the primary breadwinner, and her husband was disabled and not working.

Jane consulted a lawyer several years prior who gave her incorrect financial information about her situation. I must stress that I am not a lawyer. But, when you think about it, almost all the decisions you need to make in divorce are family and financial, not legal. I help people with all the non-legal parts of a divorce. Especially understanding the financial realities. I'm a financial advisor, divorce coach, and mediator.

When I sat down with her, she shared her lawyer's misleading advice.. Either the attorney didn't understand the situation or was not versed in the family law of that state. Where Jane lived, they capped support to avoid one person being devastated financially by supporting the other.

This counsel caused Jane to make decisions based on bad information that impacted how she lived life for the next several years. She was told by the attorney that she would have to support her disabled husband to such a degree that she wouldn't be able to afford to live independently. Waiting based on bad info also changed both the amount and duration of time she would support him.

That's a pretty extreme example of how incorrect information changes lives.

In this chapter, we will examine some of the most common myths professionals hear from people who are starting the divorce process. You may have heard it from your mom or your best friend—even looked it up on Google. That does not mean it's true! Clearing the air about some of the misconceptions can help you avoid mistakes by shifting your beliefs.

Let's look at other myths or misinformation that can cause people to make choices that aren't in their best interest.

Ten Big Myths of Divorce

1) Hire an attorney before you do anything else

2) You have to serve divorce papers on your partner, and it's best to do it first

3) Divorce is always a battle and involves a lot of fighting

4) You can choose to pay child support and figure out the amount yourselves

5) You have to have a reason (grounds) and someone needs to take the blame

6) Wives always get alimony, husbands don't

7) It's illegal to date during divorce

8) You can't control what you spend to get the divorce, the amount you pay is dictated by the lawyers and courts involved.

9) Divorce is always a financial disaster for both parties

10) Once it's over, you're done. There doesn't need to be any more connection of any kind

TEN BIG MYTHS OF DIVORCE

Myth #1: Hire an attorney before you do anything else.

It's always best to get an attorney. While consulting a lawyer is important to make sure you're on track with the legalities surrounding the divorce proceedings, mediation or counseling can also be helpful in reaching an amicable agreement between both parties.

Myth #2: You have to serve your spouse with divorce papers, and it's best if you beat them to the punch.

A lot of people think that they get the upper hand in the process somehow if they are the first ones to file. Some attorneys believe there is an advantage from a psychological point of view if you file a motion for divorce first, like a surprise attack giving you an edge over the enemy. If you catch your spouse unaware and tell them you want a divorce by serving them papers, what you've likely done is declare war. That's a pretty tricky thing to deescalate for minimal psychological advantage and probably no legal advantage.

There might be reasons to file first and have your spouse served. If there is abuse, addiction, or an extreme imbalance of power in the relationship could be examples. Even in these cases, there isn't likely a tactical benefit, but it might pave the way for other protections.

Filing first might actually be a detriment in some situations. If you've been thinking about divorce for quite some time and your partner is not aware of it for whatever reason, letting him know by being served papers sends a shot across the bow that says, "we are not doing this peacefully or collaboratively." When feeling attacked, a person's first instinct is retaliation or defense, not working together to achieve a common goal.

It may feel good for a hot second, but after that, you might find yourself backed into a strategic corner when your shocked, soon-to-be ex-spouse hires the most aggressive attorney they can and comes out swinging.

Allow space, realize what you're actually dealing with, and concentrate on making decisions based on good information with a long-term view.

Take the time to walk through the process of thinking about what might happen with each course of action you could take.

Picture this: Your spouse doesn't anticipate the news that you want a divorce. As your husband enters his office in the morning, a process server meets him at the door with the papers you've filed. He reads the documents in a partial state of shock. He had a meeting scheduled first thing and is angry and upset with not only the news that you want to divorce but by the way he learned it. He felt embarrassed in front of his peers, and it hijacked his day, making him feel anxious and out of control.

Contrast that with sitting down with him quietly and explaining how you feel. Tell him that you are scared, but you believe it's the right choice and that you will do everything possible to work with him to get through this with the greatest amount of dignity and the least amount of damage possible.

If you've read the chapter on the process options in Chapter 3, consider telling your spouse that you want a divorce personally. When you can work together to figure out the least damaging and expensive approach for your family, who files is likely incidental.

Don't get yourself caught up in the myth of thinking that all divorces start with "you've been served." That can lead to a battle from the beginning of the process and result in an entirely different outcome than working cooperatively to end your marriage.

In most cases, figuring out who will file can be a conversation well into the process rather than an aggressive move attempting to gain some domination in divorce negotiations.

Spoiler, *always* makes it a myth, but there is truth in this one. Women are the most frequent instigators of divorce. A 2015 study by the American Sociological Association (ASA) referenced in an article titled *Why Women Initiate Divorce More Often Than Men* supposes that ongoing gender inequality in home responsibilities and marital satisfaction compels more women to start the divorce process than men by a ratio of 70 percent to 30 percent.

According to Rosenfeld, the author of the ASA study, "Marriage as an institution has been a little bit slow to catch up with expectations for gender equality," Rosenfeld said. "Wives still take their husband's surnames and are sometimes pressured to do so. Husbands still expect their wives to do the bulk of the housework and the bulk of the childcare. On the other hand, I think that non-marital relationships lack the historical baggage and expectations of marriage, which makes the non-marital relationships more flexible and therefore more adaptable to modern expectations, including women's expectations for more gender equality."[13]

Myth #3: Divorce is always a battle and involves a lot of fighting.

Understand that the myth of divorce always being contentious and full of anger or rage is just that, a fairytale. This is not necessarily the case for all divorces. More often than not, the couples I work with through their divorce are sad, worried, and rightly concerned about facing the end of their marriage; they are not ready to wage war. In fact, that is one of their greatest concerns. They would prefer to come to a solution they can both live with, without spending their retirement savings or hating each other so they can move on with their lives.

13 "Women More Likely than Men to Initiate Divorces, but Not Non-Marital Breakups - American Sociological Association." 2022. American Sociological Association. September 28, 2022. https://www.asanet.org/women-more-likely-men-initiate-divorces-not-non-marital-breakups/.

It's true some may involve high levels of conflict, and those are the stories that get the most play and make the biggest impressions. Many couples can come to a mutual agreement and divorce amicably—especially if they know that it is an option from the beginning.

> Many couples are able to come to a mutual agreement and divorce amicably – especially if they know that it is an option from the beginning.

It's important to remember that just as every marriage is unique, so is every divorce. The level of conflict involved can vary greatly from one situation to another.

That's one way carefully selecting your professionals at the beginning helps you navigate the divorce process better, finding solutions that work for both parties and promoting a peaceful resolution.

Myth #4: We can choose to pay child support and the amount.

Variations of this story are common.

A couple in mediation came to their first meeting and announced that they had agreed that there would be no child support paid. In this case, the wife, Katya, was the higher earner, but the scenario works the same if you flip-flop the situation. In many ways, child support is gender neutral. Her going-to-be ex-husband, Paul, made about half of what she made. She didn't think that as a woman and mother, she should have to pay support, even with the difference in income and their plan to have the same amount of parenting time.

It was a difficult divorce after a tumultuous marriage that involved infidelity. Paul's asking for child support was making her crazy after he cheated on her and their marriage. She felt that the amount requested was unreasonable, that he was at fault for the breakdown of their marriage and shouldn't benefit from her hard-earned cash. Incensed, she said he wouldn't get a dime and that it was what he deserved after cheating on her.

Federal regulations promulgated pursuant to Title IV-D of the Social Security Act require uniform application of child support guidelines throughout a state, but each state can determine its own method of calculating support.[14]

This happens a lot. The myth here is that parents get to choose what they will pay and whether they will pay child support. In reality, the court system wants to protect the children and make sure they don't suffer unduly when parents are angry with each other. Look at it this way—did the kids do anything wrong? Should they have a lower standard of living half of the time because their dad did something that made their mom angry?

While who did what to whom can play a big role in how a divorce moves forward, it isn't usually part of the child support story. Keeping the children fed, housed, and clothed is the priority.

Myth #5: You have to have a reason (grounds), and someone needs to take the blame.

The practice of divorce might vary greatly depending on where you live because each state, and sometimes even county, has its own family law process, so I'm going to caveat this with a BIG, GIANT check on your jurisdiction. And then check it again. Use multiple sources.

14 "Child Support in the United States." 2023. Wikipedia. March 19, 2023. https://en.wikipedia.org/wiki/Child_support_in_the_United_States.

Use "the Google." Know what rules apply to you. Try hard not to get your information from someone offering more opinion and lore than fact.

You've heard it takes two to tango? One party is not always at fault—many divorces occur due to emotional, mental, or communication issues that both partners are struggling with. Our soap opera-like view of divorce supports the idea that there has to be fault, and someone needs to pay. Rather than blaming one side or another for the breakup of the marriage a reframe to how to move forward separately in a positive, productive way is warranted.

She cheated . . .

He took a job in another state and just up and left . . .

I'm so tired of them taking drugs, it's got to end . . .

These, and other reasons, CAN be used as grounds for divorce in some states, but you don't have to demonstrate and prove fault in all states. That means that all states offer some form of no-fault divorce. They may call it different things, but it's available.[15]

Many states do have a process to assign fault in the breakdown of a marriage. People may want to assign fault if the state allows leveraging blame as a reason for a greater share of the couple's assets or a bigger spousal support award.

---

15 Heineig, Melissa. n.d. "No-Fault Divorce vs. Fault Divorce FAQ." Www.nolo.com. Accessed March 24, 2023. https://www.nolo.com/legal-encyclopedia/no-fault-divorce-vs-fault-divorce-faq.html#two.

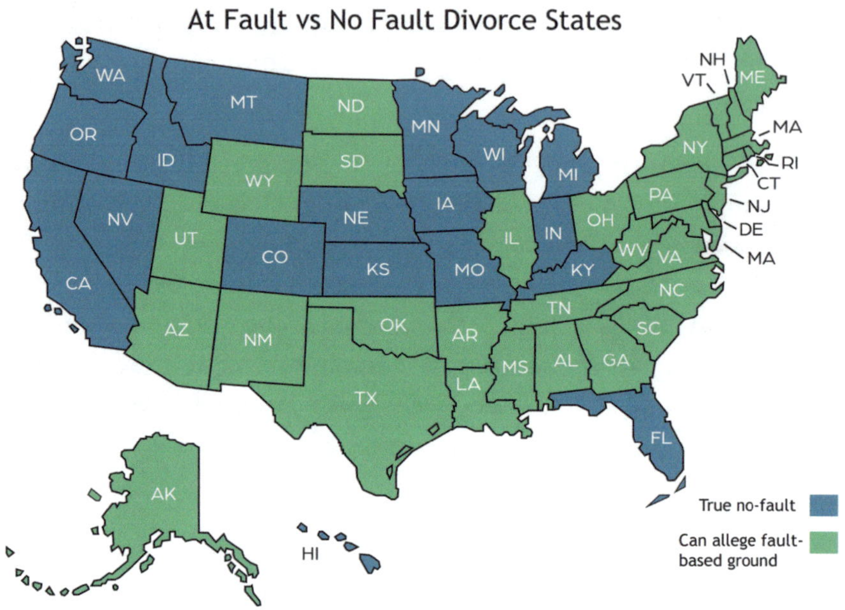

THINGS TO CONSIDER IN AN AT-FAULT STATE

While all states offer a form of no-fault divorce, in some, you have the option of assigning blame for the breakdown of the marriage and attempting to prove it in court—that is the "fault."

1. You'll need to provide evidence that your spouse is at fault for the dissolution of the marriage.

2. An at-fault divorce may take longer than a no-fault divorce, as there will be more legal procedures involved.

3. The "fault" must be one your state recognizes. Certain grounds (such as adultery or abandonment) may be necessary for you to file an at-fault divorce.

4. The type of settlement or arrangement that you receive and who pays legal costs may vary depending on which party is found liable in court.

THINGS TO CONSIDER IN A NO-FAULT STATE

Divorce in a no-fault state is often simpler and faster than an at-fault divorce. Since no one has to be found at fault for the dissolution of the marriage, couples can simply agree to the conditions of the divorce and proceed.

If infidelity is part of the reason your marriage is ending, how likely is calling that out in court going to get them the 'punishment' you think they deserve? At what cost? Most family law courts are too busy to dig deep into the wrongs done by an unfaithful partner.

More and more, assigning blame has no bearing on the case. If it does, the emphasis is on the economic impact it caused, not the emotional pain one partner suffered.

What does economic impact mean?

If the cheating spouse was spending marital funds on someone else, a judge might order that money be paid back to the marriage. Spending a couple's money on someone else in an extramarital affair is the **dissipation of marital funds**; if proven, the other spouse should be compensated for it.

Myth #6: Wives always get alimony, husbands don't.

It is a common misconception that wives always receive alimony from their husbands, while husbands do not. In reality, either spouse may be entitled to receive alimony depending on the circumstances of their marriage, their divorce, and the support laws where they are getting divorced. Polls show an upward trend in the number of women paying child support and alimony to their ex-husbands.[16] Alimony is determined on a state-by-state, in some states, case-by-case basis. Courts will examine such factors as how long the marriage lasted, each party's income, contributions to the household by either spouse, and any relevant state laws. Put simply, one gender does not automatically have an advantage over another when it comes to alimony.

Myth #7: It's illegal to date during divorce.

It isn't illegal; a 2019 study showed that 32 percent of women start dating prior to their divorce.[17] Keep in mind, it may seem inappropriate to some people and could complicate things when discussing custody arrangements and financial settlements. Especially if you're in a contested or "at-fault" divorce, it may not be a wise decision.

I've worked with divorcing couples where one or both are already dating other people as they go through the required waiting period in their state, and it doesn't even cause a ripple in their discussions. This is not the norm. More often, I've seen the tremendous strain on the process if both parties are not on board with dating other people while they are still married.

If one spouse is "swiping right" with wild abandon and the other is just feeling left behind with a broken heart, imagine how much

16 Reuters Editorial. 2019. "Business & Financial News, U.S & International Breaking News | Reuters." Reuters. 2019. https://www.reuters.com/.

17 Hogan, Allie. 2020. "This Is When You'll Be Ready to Date Post-Divorce, Research Shows." Best Life. October 6, 2020. https://bestlifeonline.com/dating-after-divorce-survey/.

more difficult talking about your parenting decisions or financial agreements may be.

Myth #8: You can't control what you spend to get the divorce; the amount you pay is dictated by the lawyers and courts involved.

Court costs and attorney fees can quickly add up, making divorce expensive and oftentimes a lengthy process depending on how much both parties agree or disagree on various issues. I think we've all heard the horror stories of divorce cases run amuck that cost the divorcing parties tens to hundreds of thousands of dollars.

The popular belief that the amount you pay to get a divorce is solely dictated by lawyers and courts is misguided. While the decisions made by legal professionals may play an important role in determining how much money a person or couple ends up spending, there are still many things that you can do to manage your expenses during this process.

For example, couples can agree on certain terms of the divorce without involving lawyers or courts, which can help keep costs lower. Additionally, couples should take particular care when hiring lawyers and other professionals and have a clear understanding of what the services are and what they will be billed for. Remember that it's not only the billing rate but also how long it takes whomever you've hired to do something. An attorney who costs $100 less an hour but takes two times as long to do something, or does it less effectively, will ultimately cost you much, much more. This is another reason to hire the correct professional for the correct job. A good divorce coach can help manage this process; making sure the right people are doing work in their area of expertise.

By being proactive and informed about the divorce process from the outset, individuals can better control their spending during a time that can be financially challenging.

Myth #9: Divorce is always a financial disaster for both parties.

People often think that divorce is going to financially ruin both parties. But that's not always the case. Sure, divorce will absolutely have financial consequences; you are taking what one household lived on and dividing it into two. Properly managed, it doesn't have to ruin both.

It really depends on a lot of factors like each person's assets and debts, their earning potential, how well they're able to negotiate a fair settlement, AND how quickly and efficiently they can come to an agreement without adding up a mountain of fees from attorneys and other professionals.

With the right help, people can make it through a divorce without devastating financial strain. One of the keys to this is reasonable goals-based settlement *instead* of who "wins" more of what the couple has.

Traditionally, women have historically had a harder time financially after divorce, often due to income disparities, time out of the workforce, and taking on more caregiving responsibilities.[18] There are some indications times are changing as more women are becoming financially independent and involved in financial decision-making. As laws around spousal support and property division shift, it's possible that more couples consider their individual and ongoing

18 United States Government Accountability Office, "The Nation's Retirement System," 2017

financial well-being should they divorce. This planning could alleviate some of the disparity seen in the standard of living when the lower-earning spouse doesn't have the opportunity or capacity to earn more.

What we are currently seeing, and a phenomenon that is only recently being talked about and researched, is the shift in the standard of living specific to women following "gray divorce." Gray divorces are defined as parties over fifty years old, and the standard of living for women divorcing after this age goes down by 45 percent, and their husband's declines by 21 percent on average.[19]

Myth #10: Once it's over, you're done. There doesn't need to be any more connection of any kind.

Although it is true that divorce often marks the end of a relationship, this does not mean that spouses will not have any further contact with one another. In some cases, there may still be practical matters such as finances or child custody issues to discuss and work out. Additionally, parties may need to come together in the future to make important decisions related to their children's welfare and well-being.

What happens when your adult children marry? What about holidays when the kids are grown up and living in different cities? Do you want to make your family decisions with an eye to the kids growing up or look at your divorce as the end of you having anything to do with your ex?

19 Lin, I-Fen, and Susan Brown. 2020. "OUP Accepted Manuscript." Journals of Gerontology Series B: Psychological Sciences and Social Sciences. https://doi.org/10.1093/geronb/gbaa157.

All of these considerations may require former spouses to maintain at least some level of connection even after their divorce is finalized. It is important for individuals going through a divorce to keep in mind that their relationship, and in some ways their commitment to one another, may continue on in some way even after they divorce.

Even after a divorce is finalized, certain financial matters may need to be discussed between the two parties. This can include things like alimony payments or adjustments, filing taxes or fixing old returns, and paying out future assets such as retirement pensions or stock options.

Individuals should try to maintain open communication with one another so that any potential disputes around finances can be handled amicably and respectfully.

CHAPTER 5 | DO THE WORK

- Read through the myths. If any of them are stories you've been operating under, do good research and find professionals who will give you the correct information.
- Are there potential myths not listed here that you are holding as truths that may impact your divorce and its outcome?

CHAPTER 5 | RESULT

I grew up with the bible school lesson of Jesus saying ***everyone who hears his words and puts them into practice is like a wise man who built his house on the rock***. Then he went on to say everyone who hears his words and does not put them into practice is ***like a foolish man who built his house on sand.***
—(Matthew 7:24-26)

Are you building the rest of your life on sand?
Or rocks?

What assumptions are underlying your decisions? Myth or reality?

- You have the ability to make decisions based on correct information AND acknowledge your emotions.

CHAPTER 5 | **HIGHLIGHTS**

- Making your plans based on false beliefs or ideas isn't sound.
- Triple check your inputs, don't just take one person's word for something.
- Acting on unsubstantiated information can cost you time, money, and emotional capital.

CHAPTER 6

A Toolbox of Touchy-Feely Yogini Shit. Namaste.

I have not ceased being fearful,
but I have ceased to let fear control me.
—Erica Jong

YOU PROBABLY SAW THIS COMING. Before I was divorced and before I was a financial advisor, I was a yoga instructor and a teacher. In versions of my life before that, I was a mom, artist, volunteer, marketer, business owner, and wife—so many things.

My guess is as you look back on your life, you've been so many things as well, and they all will inform the decisions you're faced with making as you go through a divorce.

One of the primary drivers in creating this book was looking around and seeing that most of the resources fell into one of two buckets. Either they were about how to make wise and logical financial decisions, or they were about how to navigate the mental and emotional shifts that happen in your life during a divorce.

MONEY AND EMOTIONS ARE NOT SEPARATE

I want to share some thoughts about tools you can use that will help you be in a better mental and emotional place to make serious financial decisions.

Looking at all the financial decisions that need to be made and knowing that often they are colored by emotions and the baggage we carry after participating in a marriage for many years, I don't think the financial decisions can be, nor should be, separated from emotions and mindset. This toolbox is separated into three sections.

1. Well-being
2. Tools for meetings
3. Thoughts for moving forward

The first, overall reminder, is to prioritize caring for yourself. Kate Northrup says, "Body first, business second." You can't make good decisions from a place of poor health or imbalance. The second is tactical methods that may help you get through divorce meetings if that's difficult for you, as it was for me. Last, keep your eye on the future as you reshape it.

> When we truly care for ourselves,
> it becomes possible to care about other people.
> —Eda LeShan

WELL-BEING (AKA SELF-CARE)

We throw the word *self-care* around as though it's as easy as ordering a happy meal. It's overused and watered down. In some crazy way, it has come to be identified with indulgences like manicures and massages instead of taking a deep look at what is in our best interests to live a complete, healthy, balanced life.

Any one of these self-care solutions may or may not resonate with you, and that's OK. It's an individual journey. I'm sharing the things I've found that have helped both my clients and me come to a better place to make decisions, as well as recognizing the filters that can impact those decisions. If these don't work for you, keep seeking self-care solutions until you find things that do.

Here is my non-comprehensive list that might jog ideas or inspiration for how you can take good care of yourself as you navigate your own divorce in your own way.

Therapy

One of the first things that I did when my husband announced his leaving was to make an appointment for my children to see a therapist. That did not turn out as I intended or planned, and here's why.

I was doing what I always did. Participating in a form of avoidance that I misinterpreted as efficiency and productivity. One of my things was to make sure my kids received proper support right away. The wise therapist I took them to explained to me afterward that I was actually doing more damage than good. By rushing them to a mental health professional, she explained, I made them see change was happening, right now, and it was very real. Kids want to hold on to the normalcy of their old life as long as they possibly can. Marching them into a therapist's office forced something that they both were not ready to face and hadn't experienced the emotions of yet. It was too early.

At the same time, I wasn't taking care of my own mental health. I'd gone to therapy many times in my life, but this time—when I probably most needed it—I was too busy trying to get through the days and nights to get help.

Nancy Hetrick, a CDFA® and mentor, said to me, after watching me play out my patterns in business, "This is where you hide." She was referring to my excuses about why I couldn't do the things I said I was going to do or make my big dreams come true. I was just too busy in divorce. To this day I have the post-it note that says *this is where you hide* watching me from my computer. I wrote it during that conversation as my forever reminder that diversion doesn't help me or anyone else. I was so busy with "to-dos" and checklists I wasn't taking care of myself at all. I went back to therapy the next week.

There are many types of therapy -

Cognitive Behavioral Therapy (CBT)

Dialectical Behavior Therapy (DBT)

Psychoanalytic Therapy

Interpersonal Therapy (IPT)

Internal Family Systems

Mindfulness-Based Cognitive Therapy (MBCT)

Eye Movement Desensitization and Reprocessing (EMDR)

Neuro-Linguistic Programming (NLP)

Art Therapy, Music Therapy, Play Therapy

What I found worked wonders for me was EMDR. It's a psychotherapy treatment that was founded originally by Francine Shapiro to recognize and heal the distress associated with traumatic memories.[20]

This might not be your flavor. This section is really more about having the openness to identify if you would benefit from outside support and not giving up until you find the kind of help that works for you.

Realize that what you need now might shift over time. I participated in EMDR to help me move out of being reactive to things that triggered traumatic memories so I could clear them and move on to being more present. Now I'm finding that NLP (Neuro-Linguistic Programming) and working through Internal Family Systems is helpful in my ongoing healing.

Money note: Check into your communities' resources if your finances are tight. If you are looking at mental health support as an indulgence you can't afford from a time or money perspective, there might be resources there that support you. I used Family Service Center in my area to get income-based sliding scale fees I could afford.

Support Groups

There have been a plethora of new support groups finding their way into our world available on social media. I don't know if some of this is a fallout from the years of being isolated through COVID or if it's an idea whose time has come. I will throw out a caution flag, some

20 "Francine Shapiro, Ph.D. | EMDR Institute – EYE MOVEMENT DESENSITIZATION and REPROCESSING THERAPY." 2019. Emdr.com. 2019. https://www.emdr.com/francine-shapiro-ph-d/.

of these groups seem to have evolved into either the digital form of the dinner party I attended or a place where professionals stalk prospective clients.

You are affected by those you surround yourself with. Know that if you're tuned into a place where all the stories are negative, that's likely going to rub off on you. Try to be discriminating about where you spend your time; follow your intuition—are they helping or selling? Does this help you feel better or worse?

DivorceCare® and Second Saturday®

These are well-known, national support groups. I went to DivorceCare within months of my husband leaving, seeking support. Although strictly against the rules, it had a dating service vibe. There was a trying to get together, out of class for coffee, or a meal that felt much more like "let's get together (wink)" than let's process this thing that's happening. This was absolutely not what I needed at the time. That is only my experience in the group I joined; others may be very different.

Second Saturday is education-oriented. Know that it is run by professionals who pay for licensing of the name to operate the seminars in hopes of finding clients. I participated in this as well, but as a professional rather than someone going through a divorce. In my experience, they are good-hearted, and the emphasis is on providing helpful information; the ulterior motive is finding clients. Not good, not bad . . . just important to keep in mind.

There is a divorce instruction center near where I used to live that offers information and seminars. Same thing, there's pay-to-play going on among divorce professions that are not divulged to clients. The only professionals who presented were those who paid for the sponsorship, but that payment was never disclosed to the attendees. They believe the facility has curated people to help them. Not so.

Why do I tell you this? Simply ask the question. What is the motivation of the group you're looking for support from? Did someone pay to be able to talk with you? What are their qualifications beyond that?

The internet is your friend, do research and try out different options. And, try not to get discouraged if the first one or two or ten that you dip your toe into don't feel quite right. There is a group out there for you.

Faith-Based Support

Hopefully, this has evolved since I went through my divorce.

The second call I made, after calling my best friend, was to my Deacon at the church I'd attended for decades. I was highly involved in the church, the Elder of Children's Ministries, for many years. I had volunteered in everything from running Sunday School to the Christmas pageant, from cooking dinner for homeless families at the church to working funeral receptions when we lost someone. I honestly expected the full support of my church. What I got was next to nothing.

In retrospect, I think that they just weren't equipped to provide me with the support that I needed. There is an inherent amount of cognitive dissonance in providing someone going through divorce support. We are not supposed to divorce if we've promised: "Til death do us part."

I hope this has changed, and if you participate in organized religion, you are able to find support in whatever house you worship in. I've said it many times, I'm not an advocate of divorce, and I don't wish it on anyone.

We need to examine the number of people divorcing in our society and realize that it happens and will continue to happen. Based on CDC data, including divorce rate trends through 2021, there are about four divorces for every ten marriages annually.[21]

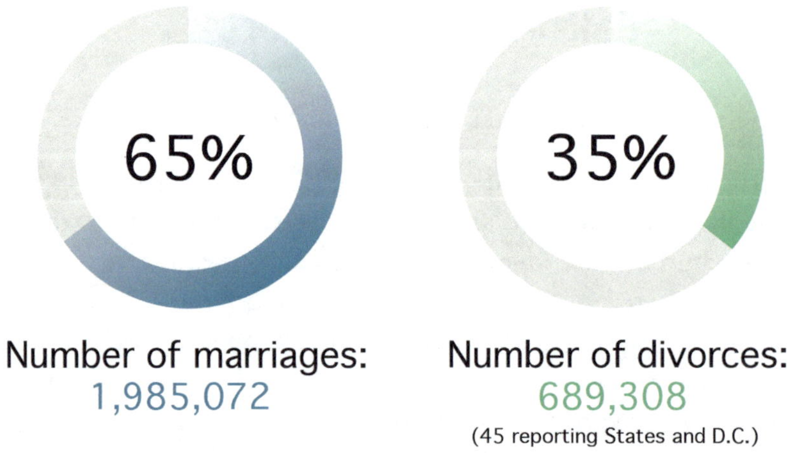

Religion seems to play a role in these numbers. The rate of divorce between religious and nonreligious women was reviewed and is slightly lower for those practicing a religion.[22] Slightly. The annual

21 CDC. 2019. "FastStats - Marriage and Divorce." Centers for Disease Control and Prevention. 2019. https://www.cdc.gov/nchs/fastats/marriage-divorce.htm.
22 Stone, Lyman. 2021. "The Religious Marriage Paradox: Younger Marriage, Less Divorce." Institute for Family Studies. December 15, 2021. https://ifstudies.org/blog/the-religious-marriage-paradox-younger-marriage-less-divorce.

divorce rate among married women with a nonreligious upbringing is around 5 percent. For religious women, it's around 4.5 percent.

We can look at a lot of statistics in many different ways. They all point to divorce continuing and being both damaging and expensive.

Ignoring it and not dealing with it will not make it any better. Trying to understand it and lessen the effect on families will make a huge difference in our communities' future well-being. We need to talk about this and come up with creative solutions that acknowledge the role of religion in marriage and the commitments while also allowing for the fact that divorce does and will continue to happen.

I believe that it is much more productive for a church to provide needed support for the families as they go through this difficult transition instead of turning their back on them. I stopped attending that church after about a year of actively trying to get support through Stephen Ministry, my Deacon, and attending services.

If your faith plays an important role in your life, I deeply and sincerely hope that you find the support that you need. If you are not receiving that care, I hope that you find a place that will provide it.

Caring for Your Physical Body

As the activities I used to do fell away, and I found myself working more and sleeping less, stressing more, and moving less, I stopped exercising as I was accustomed to. I'm sure that added to a downward spiral.

Try to get good sleep. It's not an indulgence. If you find that you're not sleeping, see what methods you can employ to help you with that. It is something I still struggle with, but it's getting better. Simple, little aids like magnesium or warm golden milk before bed and a sound machine help me. My partner, Patrick, got me a weighted blanket for my last birthday, and I love that. I no longer watch television in the evening, it doesn't work for me.

I've embarked on a new journey to clean up my eating; I didn't think my diet was too bad, but I'm feeling a huge benefit from concentrating on it even more. I've had all my overdue checkups that fell by the wayside in my money and time-starved years during and immediately after my divorce.

What makes you feel better in your body? Do that!

You deserve to be taken care of, especially when you are the one doing the caretaking.

Mindfulness Practice

> Some of my personal favorite meditation apps are 10% Happier, Grace, Calm and Oura.

Mindfulness practice can be beneficial when going through a divorce as it allows you to take a step back from the situation and provide yourself with some clarity and perspective. Taking time to pause and engage your senses in breath or body scans helps to lessen the impact of stress and anxiety related to the divorce process. Mindfulness can also help reduce the tendency to dwell on things that happened in the past, a kind of retelling of your own story in your head over and over again. Becoming more present in the moment can help you leave the old stories behind and create space to invent your new life.

There are many apps out there you can use as tools when you find yourself in moments of fear, scarcity, or agitation. Some of my personal favorites are *10% Happier, Grace, and Calm*. Each of these has a different take on meditation and can help readjust a spiraling thought process within minutes. There's a ton of research out there about how beneficial meditation is. If you're in a space where your monkey mind has taken over, a guided meditation from one of these apps may be just the ticket to help calm your system. Keep trying until you find one that suits you.

There's a huge benefit to living in the present, from better sleep to reduced anxiety. I truly believe it can help you heal from divorce more readily.[23]

---

23 "Mindfulness for Your Health." 2021. NIH News in Health. June 1, 2021. https://newsinhealth.nih.gov/2021/06/mindfulness-your-health#:~:text=Health%20Benefits%20of%20Mindfulness&text=Mindfulness%2Dbased%20treatments%20have%20been.

Mindfulness Practice Ideas

Affirmations

Breathwork

Focus on something in your environment

Guided Meditation

Walking Meditation

Body Scan

Gratitude Practice

Take a Social Media Time Out

Taking regular breaks from social media platforms and news outlets can give you a break on two counts.

Social media often shows the bright shiny side of things, sugar-coating people's lives. If you're spending time looking at how great everyone in your circle of contacts is showing up as it might cast a bigger shadow on your situation than need be. Staying away from social media can help avoid comparing your situation to others who may look better. I have no proof, just a gut feeling, my ex-husband spent an awful lot of time the year before he said he wanted a divorce unemployed and scrolling Facebook. We had a flawed relationship, but Facebook didn't end it. I do think it contributed greatly to his dissatisfaction with our marriage because he was comparing it to how wonderful his Facebook friends' lives seemed to be.

News is often littered with stories and accounts of other couples' divorces. This can be stressful and overwhelming, leading to further anxiety and negative emotions. Taking the time to disconnect from these sources can help create a much-needed respite from constant reminders of divorce-related content. If it doesn't bring you peace and renewal, consider turning it off.

Spend Time with Those Who Build You Up

Spending time with friends, family, animals, or in nature can be deeply healing during the divorce process. Taking part in activities with people you love and trust will help foster positive relationships and lift your spirits when going through a difficult time. Connecting with nature is also particularly beneficial, as it provides an important reminder of your own strength and resilience. Being in nature or with supportive friends can provide a sense of comfort and solace, allowing you to feel held despite the challenges of divorce.

I am forever grateful to my family and three specific friends who held me up and built me up during my divorce. Find your people and make a practice of spending time with them. Even if you're down, they will understand because they love you.

TOOLS FOR MEETINGS

Meetings with your going-to-be ex, your attorney, courtroom hearings—they can all be incredibly taxing. For years I had a visceral response when I was in the presence of or had to speak to my ex-husband. I would shake, visibly, out-of-control trembling. Being affected so dramatically made it hard for me to concentrate on the topics at hand. It's hard to think about financial settlements or holiday schedules when you're quaking.

These are some of the things I've used or recommended to clients if they find themselves unsettled during meetings.

Build in a Buffer Zone

Schedule time before and time after the meeting so you can gather yourself without feeling as anxious or stressed. If you're a fan of mindfulness practice, consider checking in with a guided meditation for ten minutes before the scheduled start. Even ten minutes of music you love can make a world of difference.

Plan a Post-Meeting Session

I learned this from my divorce coach, and it was incredibly helpful. I scheduled time after our Collaborative team meetings to debrief with a supportive friend or my dogs. Knowing that scheduled time was on the other side helped me keep my cool when things got heated and gave me space to transition back into whatever responsibility was on the other side, whether it was a work meeting or making dinner.

Play Games

Sounds silly, doesn't it? Give it a try. This was one of the most useful tools I implemented, and I've shared it with countless people since then. Another divorce coach shared the concept with me when I explained how frustrated I was during our meetings when certain things happened, like being talked about as though I wasn't in the room or being demeaned.

Her suggestion was that if I was sure that this thing, this predictive behavior, was going to happen, rather than become angered and frustrated when it did, simply turn it into a game. So say that I knew at some point the conversation would turn to talk about me as though I wasn't there. For example, "she has trouble sticking with a job, she doesn't stick to anything," or "she's not doing her fair share of contributing financially. I'm tired of holding her up."

Instead of becoming defensive and explaining myself or rising to the bait, I would just make a small bet with myself before the meeting as to how long it would take before the expected behavior would occur. So if it were an hour-long meeting, I might say, in minute twenty-three I can expect to be referred to as "she," as if I weren't there. And then, I would concentrate on watching the clocks and seeing when the first time happened. There really wasn't a prize, but it did distract me from becoming emotionally engaged or taking the bait in something that was triggering to me.

How can you use this? If you find yourself reacting negatively to something that is triggering either in the present or because it's repeated behavior that showed up in the patterns of your marriage, try to think of a way to turn that into a game. For some reason, it helps take it out of being a personal attack and makes you more of an observer than the victim.

If you find something triggers you, see if you can turn it into a game to blunt the impact. Make yourself an observer instead of a target.

Tapping

Tapping, also known as Emotional Freedom Technique (EFT), is an evidence-based practice that helps to reduce stress and anxiety. It involves focusing on specific emotions or thought patterns while lightly tapping on various points of the body with your fingertips. This type of tapping helps to reset the body's energy systems, improving its ability to cope with stress and find emotional balance. By releasing stuck energy, tapping can help you reconnect with positive thoughts and emotions, helping you feel empowered and supported through difficult times such as divorce. You can use this technique subtly during meetings if you feel the need for a reset.

Breathing Techniques

I love these because they can be done both before or after meetings and oftentimes in plain sight. When you take control of your breath, it helps stabilize the energy in the body, which, in turn, helps you make more thoughtful and sound decisions. Some of these might be more overt, and some might work better for you than others. You can certainly find many options on YouTube that will walk you through how to use these exercises. Here's just one example:

Box breathing is a simple yet powerful technique used to reduce stress and anxiety. It involves slowly inhaling for four counts, holding the breath for four counts, exhaling for four counts, and then holding the breath again for four counts. This practice helps to regulate the body's breathing cycle and slow down the heart rate, allowing it to enter a relaxed state more easily. Through this practice, it is possible to promote relaxation and clarity of thought, creating space to focus on yourself during difficult times.

If you're not finding things that serve you in this list, reach out to our Facebook group or dig into the internet or watch uplifting YouTube videos. There is something out there that will make your journey smoother.

Join the Bridging Divorce Facebook group here:

https://www.facebook.com/groups/128097150218422

Use a Worry Stone

A worry stone is a small, smooth stone or pebble that is often used as a stress-relief tool. The practice of using worry stones dates back to ancient Greece, where people would rub smooth stones called "fidget stones" to help reduce anxiety and promote relaxation.

Worry stones are typically small enough to fit in the palm of your hand and have a smooth, flat surface that feels soothing when rubbed with your thumb. They can be made from a variety of materials, including gemstones, crystals, and even wood or metal.

The idea behind using a worry stone is that it provides a physical sensation that helps to distract the mind from anxious thoughts and promotes feelings of calmness and relaxation. Some people also believe that certain types of stones or crystals have healing properties that can enhance their calming effects.

Moving Forward

In time you might find yourself wanting to move beyond the tactical things that will help you get through the process. The primary area I see helping people move beyond divorce, with grace, is forgiveness. Of yourself and, if you choose, others. A big part of moving forward is recognizing where you are and the direction you'd like to head.

Moving through Emotions

I center this on *forgiveness.* I tried to make peace with the concept often at the beginning of my divorce, and I see others grapple with it regularly. I found over the years that when I let things sit and don't expect too much, as a concept, it becomes much more palatable. My choice was to let go of the concept of forgiveness or the need to forgive, and instead move into the practice of non-attachment and radical acceptance.

One of the things we expect of ourselves or others is to leapfrog from really negative feelings to high-level positive ones. To be very hurt or distrustful or angry and then expect to be joyful is not realistic.

I advocate that you just try to get to the next level. Below you'll see the Emotional Guidance Scale from Abraham-Hicks.

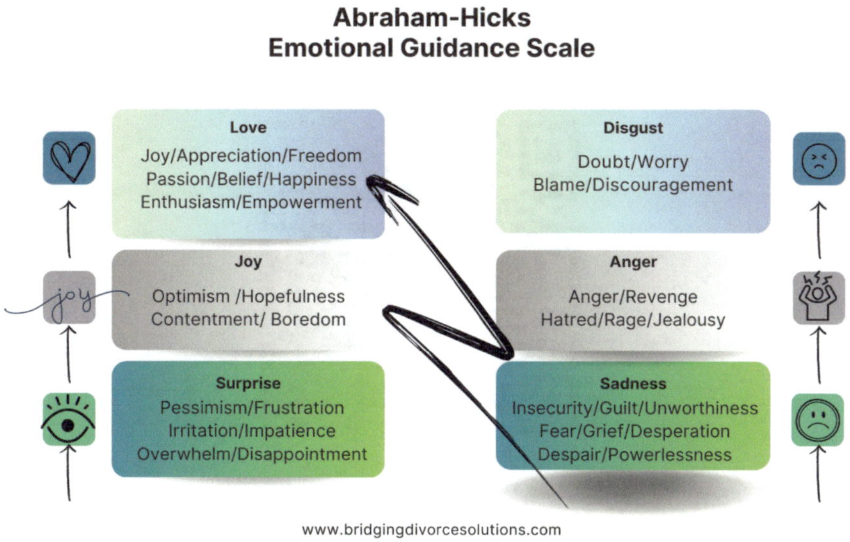

How to use the Emotional Scale: Name where you are and pick a level or two up. Concentrate on moving into that space, jealousy to anger is movement in the right direction. So is pessimism to hope.

If you bypass the thought of forgiveness, which is "other" based, and concentrate on identifying where you are and what you want to move into, I believe you will find progress more quickly and authentically. If you're sitting in rage or denial and expecting yourself to get to joy right away, the likelihood is low. You're putting yourself in a position where you haven't met the expectations you set for yourself, which can be depressing as well. But if you're sitting in rage and you just want to get to anger, that's a doable step. It's progress and achievable.

Moving step by step releases the pressure and acknowledges how you feel. I've gotten into the practice of giving each of my clients an emotion chart that helps them identify where they are and where they want to be but also helps show them that any progress is progress and expectations don't have to be tremendously high to be positive movement. If you'd like to print out your own, here's a link where you can download the PDF.[24]

https://bridgingdivorcesolutions.com/abraham-hicks-emotional-scale/

Give Yourself Space to Change and Shift and Grow

Last year I enrolled in another yoga teacher training, thinking that it would compel me to go back to yoga. I had a regular practice and was looking forward to building my teaching work, and enjoying it tremendously before my husband lost his job and divorce followed.

What I've realized in the years since is that there's no going back. Those classes were interesting and beneficial, but not the fix I intended when I signed up for them. I'm a different person, and I'm in a different place. Anytime I find myself trying to go back, it tends to trip me up.

24 Bernstein, Gabby. 2020. "How to Use the Abraham-Hicks Emotional Guidance Scale." Gabby Bernstein. February 2, 2020. https://gabbybernstein.com/emotional-guidance-scale-abraham-hicks/.

As long as I'm in touch with myself and forward moving, accepting myself, and acknowledging where I am in this time, I am so much more likely to be in an accepting state or a state of flow than if I'm trying to force behavior on myself or return to a person I once was.

There's the old saying that you can't step in the same river twice, and in many ways, I think that's true. I was trying to go back in time and recapture pieces of myself when I'm an entirely different human now. And finally, realizing that has freed me up to enjoy my yoga practice again in a different way and on a different level.

Think about where can you give yourself space without expecting that you'll return to what once was, but allowing yourself to step into something that's good for you, that you enjoy, that fills you up.

> "No woman ever steps in the same river twice, for it is not the same river and she is not the same woman." Heraclitus (OK, he said "man," I think it needed to be changed up.)

I understand that all marriages that end in divorce don't travel this path. I've worked with some couples who divorce with the dignity and grace I aspired to when I started the process.

CHAPTER 6 | DO THE WORK

- Take some time to assess your triggers and come up with a game plan for how you can work around them. Experiment with different techniques.
- Are there areas where you are not taking care of yourself? Are you getting enough sleep? Eating good food? Identify the ways you are and are not taking care of yourself. Make small changes on a regular basis to replace harmful activities with good self-care.

CHAPTER 6 | RESULTS

In the midst of chaos and pain,
When your heart feels shattered and drained,
Remember to take a moment for you,
To practice self-care, to renew.

Take a deep breath, let it out slow,
Feel the tension in your body go.
Find a quiet place where you can be alone,
And let yourself simply moan.

Cry if you need to, scream if you must,
Letting out emotions is a healthy trust.
Write in your journal or read a good book,
Focus on healing and how far you've come, look.

Take a walk in nature, feel the sun on your face,
Connect with the world and find some grace.
Meditate, do yoga, calm your mind,
Allow yourself to unwind.

Self-care during divorce may seem like a chore,
But it's essential for healing and so much more.
So be kind to yourself, love yourself true,
And remember that this too shall pass for you.

- The biggest result: you'll make better decisions and recover more quickly if you tend to yourself.

CHAPTER 6 | **HIGHLIGHTS**

- There are many things that are out of control in the divorce process, especially if you're using litigation.
- Recognizing things that may get in the way of the process that is in your control, and coming up with a game plan that puts you in a conscious decision-making mode instead of a reactionary place **before** that's triggered will help.

PART II: FAMILY AND FRIENDS

I sustain myself with the love of family.
—Maya Angelou

CHAPTER 7

Family First. Really. All Family.

Daring to set boundaries is about having the courage to love ourselves even when we risk disappointing others.
—Brené Brown

DIVORCE CREATES A NEWLY SHAPED FAMILY, whether you have children or not.

Here, I'll share a couple of my challenges over the years. This share is in the hope that you can start looking at your life and your family's lives with an eye on the future. A vision of the future you would like far beyond divorce.

Most recently, I traveled to Chicago over the Christmas holiday because all three of my children were going to be there, two of them with their significant others, one of whom I'd never met. They were staying with my ex-husband, and I gave a lot of thought as to whether I should go or not.

I talked to them about me skipping that trip and arranging to see them all at some other time that wouldn't be so busy and where they wouldn't have the potential conflict of building in time to see me along with the time with their father, his side of the family and their friends.

As it turned out, I saw all three of my kids only once for a couple of hours and two of them for a couple of hours individually. It made me extremely sad. I spent Christmas day waiting for them to come over for a feast of food I'd spent the morning preparing. The day wore on, and when it became evident they wouldn't come, I spent the rest of Christmas sobbing as we cleaned up the food and departed for the airport that afternoon. Just before I left, I briefly saw and hugged my sons good-bye in a parking lot before we hopped into the Lyft to the airport with my daughter. Somehow, those ten minutes felt even worse.

In retrospect, I should have been clearer. I thought they were coming. They said they would visit us where we were staying in an Evanston condo. Later, I learned they thought I just suggested they stop by and that Pat's family was coming over, so it wasn't a big deal. So they didn't come. My understanding was that would be the other time I could spend with them the week we were there, meet my son's new girlfriend, and visit with all of them together again. I was heartbroken not to see them.

The next day I got a text from my ex-sister-in-law telling me how much she enjoyed seeing my kids (they are fantastic), how proud I must be of them (always) what amazing adults they'd turned into (absolutely true).

I didn't respond to her for weeks, not because I disagreed. They are lovely human beings, and I miss them all the time. Because I was so sad about not having seen my children more. And, hard as it is to admit, I was resentful that she got to spend pretty much the same time with my children as I did. And it was the first time she'd reached out to me in years. After the divorce, I'd occasionally contacted her and her sister to stay in touch and to suggest getting together for lunch or coffee. They always said it would be a great idea; we should do that . . . later. They were busy.

Before our divorce was final, and months into the process, my niece on my husband's side was getting married (it's funny, autocorrect wants that to read "my husband's niece," but she was my niece, too, for her whole life up until then). An invitation to the wedding and a bridal shower beforehand arrived.

The shower was the first time I'd encountered that side of the family I'd been part of for decades, other than a phone call to my sister-in-law trying to understand what was happening the week my husband left. I was nervous. I didn't know how to behave in this new role. I hoped they wouldn't treat me differently.

Almost as soon as I arrived at the shower, one of the other guests, an aunt of my niece, came up to me and said, "I can't believe I'm seeing you here. I can't believe you were invited after what *you did*."

I had no response. I wasn't prepared for that hostility. I put on the best happy face I could manage and made small talk with others. Making it through the rest of that shower was excruciating for me.

Not long after, I was at one of my daughter's softball tournaments on a hot, dusty June day when I got a call from my sister-in-law, the bride's mother. Again, the reason for her reaching out stunned me. She'd called to un-invite me to my niece's wedding. She said it would be best for everyone if I didn't attend. I stood in that middle space where the four fields of the tournament intersected, surrounded by people I didn't know. Softball fans cheered around me as I cried when she told me my presence would ruin the wedding.

I'd vacationed with these families, hosting and attending holiday celebrations for decades. We built a house on the same lake in Wisconsin to see them more. I knew things would change, but I did not expect to be completely ostracized, especially since I wasn't the one leaving the marriage.

But I was and am. Except for that same niece, who stayed caring. I did attend her wedding, but just the ceremony so I could watch her get married and tell her how beautiful she was. I didn't stay for the reception.

I see now how not putting the care I could have into looking at the whole family long-term puts my children in the unenviable place of picking sides. Even if it's not stated outright, it's the outcome. And likely to affect them and their children for years.

As mentioned elsewhere, I've tried to move past this with my ex multiple times. From trying to have conversations about how we each have our stories, and who is right or "wins" doesn't matter anymore. What does matter is how our kids are being affected. And the impact on any event in the future—engagements, weddings, grandchildren, funerals. All of these are under the strain of the unfortunate condition of our divorce and the post-divorce relationship.

That's how divorce has played out in my family. I'm sharing this to give you an example of how decisions you make now in your divorce can impact your lives forever in unintended ways.

In the rest of Part II: Family and Friends, we'll look at:

- **L**etting friends and family support you through this process (Chapter 8)
- Ways to focus on your family's future (Chapter 9)
- Practicalities of building a Parenting Plan (Chapter 10)
- Dealing with traditions and firsts (Chapter 11)
- A toolbox to help with moving your family positively through a divorce (Chapter 12)

CHAPTER 7 | DO THE WORK

- Sit with how you want landmark events in your family's future, tomorrow and years down the road, to play out. Journal or vision board or write a letter to your future self or children about this.

CHAPTER 7 | RESULT

Can you look beyond how messed up and confusing things might be today and focus on what you'd like them to be in the future?

Write about your friends and family in the future:

- You'll have fewer regrets and better relationships if you keep future-focused and develop clear goals and communications.

CHAPTER 7 | **HIGHLIGHTS**

- Thinking beyond today's decisions in your divorce can make a great deal of difference for you and your kids, and yes, your ex.
- Divorce for families is not just completing your state's required Parenting Plan; some other considerations can be incredibly important areas to walk through as you split.
    - Long-standing family relationships
    - Communicating with friends and family in the process
    - Holidays and traditions
    - Future landmark events like weddings and graduations

CHAPTER 8

Friends and Family—Asking for Help and Hugs

A real friend is one who walks in when the rest of the world walks out.
—Walter Winchell

FROM THE BEGINNING OF YOUR JOURNEY, you will need support and understanding. Often people don't know how to give it; they don't know what to say, and they may get caught up in the drama and make things worse without knowing. This chapter addresses ways for you to ask for support clearly and thoughtfully.

You can ask for what you need and actively pursue the care you need, which involves communicating it to the people important to you. It's going to make you saner and more supported. And when you and your family are in a better place, you will inevitably make better decisions.

Not only did I lose my entire family of in-laws in my divorce, but I also lost many friends. These were also people we'd vacationed with, ushered in many New Year's with, had "empty the fridge" potlucks with, and simply enjoyed life with.

I don't know if it would have been any different if I'd been better able to communicate what I needed. Hell, if I'd better understood what I needed. I can't help but think it would have.

What I experienced was a few steady, stalwart souls stepped up and supported me. I don't mean by taking sides; I mean they intuitively knew that just being there was helping. They checked in on me to see how I was doing. They showed they cared.

What I experienced more was that friends dropped me. Neighbors didn't include me in things I went to before. It was as if Brenda didn't exist, if she was not part of a married couple. Part of this was that people didn't know what to do with me. I believe some of it was if we were going through this crazy, ugly thing, it could happen to them too. It was just too close for comfort. My presence became frightening.

> *Look to Chapter 13 for thoughts on assembling professionals to help you through a divorce, individually if you're going the court route or as a couple if you choose Mediation or the Collaborative Process.*

And I was so scared.

While working on her financial plans, a new client recently described how shocked she was when, close to a year after her divorce was final, she got an invoice from her attorney for over $10,000 that she'd not billed. Yes, she was shocked when she got the bill so late. What stuck with her was, as she put it, "I thought she was my friend. All of those phone calls. I trusted her. I thought we were just talking. I had no idea she would charge me for them."

Separating your personal needs from your professional support will get you a better outcome and cost you less money. Acknowledging and planning for what those needs are will keep you more whole.

PERSONAL SUPPORT

> When the world is so complicated, the simple gift of friendship is within all of our hands.
> Maria Shriver

You know you're more likely to get what you need if you can ask for it. You may think the people who love you will automatically know that and be there without saying. They might not; they may be afraid to approach you or concerned about saying the wrong thing. Reflecting on everything I wished I'd done differently in my divorce, one of those was that I wanted to have been a better communicator with friends and family about what I needed. I was likely to cry and panic, which could have pushed people away. Who wants to be around someone who constantly appears to be on the verge of a breakdown?

This letter resembles what I wish I'd shared with my friends and family during my divorce. Perhaps a version of it will serve you.

A LETTER ABOUT HOW TO HELP AND SUPPORT ME

Dear (person I need support from),

I wanted to reach out to you because I am going through a difficult time right now—I am getting a divorce. This is not something I ever thought would happen to me, and it's proving to be an incredibly emotional and challenging experience.

One of the hardest things about going through a divorce is feeling like nobody understands what I am going through. Maybe they don't know what to say, so they say nothing. It can be frustrating to need support and know that you, who are so important to me, might not know what to say or how to react, even though you mean well.

That's why I wanted to share what I would love and some things that don't make me feel better.

It would feel good if:

- *You checked in to see how I am; if I say "fine," ask me more than once.*
- *You want to talk about things we talked about before this started. It helps me feel more normal.*
- *You can listen when I need to decompress without feeling like you need to fix things or judge me.*
- *You let me know if I'm acting bitter or negative. I know it sneaks out, BUT that's not the person I want to be.*

It doesn't feel good when:

- *You don't invite me to things you would have if I were not getting divorced.*
- *You only want to talk about the drama and trauma of divorce.*
- *You compare my situation to others, especially if they turned out badly.*
- *You think I can do all of the things I did before. I need some help keeping up with parenting, work, volunteering, and going through all the divorce stuff.*

I ask for your support and understanding during this time. Even if you don't have personal experience with divorce, just being there for me and listening when I need to talk can make a huge difference. ***And if you're unsure what to say, that's OK too—sometimes acknowledging that things are tough and that you care can be enough.***

I also want you all to know I am still the person you've always known and loved. Divorce doesn't define me, and it doesn't change who I am at my core. So please don't feel like you have to tiptoe around or treat me differently—I'm still the same friend (sister-in-law, aunt) you've always had.

Thank you so much for reading this letter and for your continued love and support during this difficult time. It means more than words can express.

With love,

[Your Name]

Some people will fall away, and some will draw near. You'll make new friends and probably have new relationships in your new life. Consider who it is that it's important to you to keep, and make an effort to do so.

Consider asking one or two particularly supportive and spectacular friends or family to provide normalcy. Maybe it's going to a movie regularly or getting a manicure. Perhaps you have always golfed, and the golf club membership got axed as part of what you're going through. Will old friends meet you for a round at a public course?

CHAPTER 8 | DO THE WORK

- Make a list of the people you want support from (an important distinction, this is NOT to "be on your side" or force them to take a side).
- Make a list of the top three to five relationships from your comprehensive list.
- Reach out to at least 3 to 5 people and ask for their understanding and support. Be clear about what that means to you. Maybe using a version of my letter or one you put together based on how you need to be held and supported through your divorce.
- Brainstorm the best way to communicate with the people who are important to you.
- Understand if people are not comfortable and can't commit, move on.

CHAPTER 8 | RESULTS

How much better will you feel if you know you have a few people who can give you the support you need when you need it?

Who are your people? (Make sure they know.)

- You will have a few people dedicated to supporting you and how you need to support through your divorce.
- You won't leave friendships and family members as fallout of your divorce without thinking or trying to keep essential relationships.

CHAPTER 8 | **HIGHLIGHTS**

- Stress negatively impacts the ability to make good decisions. Not having good support leads to increased stress.
- Being active and thoughtful about asking for support means you are more likely to get it.
- Some people will feel like they want or need to take sides. If you can steer clear of that, you will be less likely to engage in a win/lose mentality and more likely to stay goal based.

CHAPTER 9

Focus on your Family's Future

Choose to focus your time, energy and conversation around people who inspire you, support you and help you to grow you into your happiest, strongest, wisest self.
—Karen Salmansohn

WHAT ARE THE ELEMENTS that were important to you in your marriage? What are the things you have a hard time letting go of? How might you reshape your vision of the future as a married family to a post-divorce family? In this chapter, I'll coach you to orient your thinking and, accordingly, your decisions about your future.

Focus on life beyond the finalization of divorce is often not thought of too much as married couples separate into two households. They work out the operational facts, but future thinking is left by the wayside. This is particularly true when attorneys negotiate for their clients to settle divorce terms.

Think about it, when done well, they will have no future contact with their clients post-divorce. Their job is to get you over the finish line. Many look at "divorce is done" as the finish line, but I contend that this is the starting line for the rest of your life. This should be the focus. Those conversations rarely discuss what you want your children's wedding to look like or how your family dynamic will look like when you're in the same room together in ten years. You should do this before you decide who's paying for soccer and who gets them on Christmas.

Losing focus on the future was my biggest mistake and greatest regret. The process of divorce can keep you tied up in the trauma and fear of the moment. I believe it would have been life-changing if my professionals and support system had coached me around **what I want life to look like for my children and me with more vision and less of a tactical approach.** Both in how I moved through the process and where I focused on making decisions.

This chapter is notably brief. It's about identifying what you want; no one else can do that for you. It's important. Would life be different if you tried preserving relationships with your former spouse and/or in-laws, stepchildren, or mutual friends?

CHAPTER 9 | DO THE WORK

- Reimagine what you want special dates in the future to look like when you are no longer married. Be as graphic and explicit as possible. Is it a graduation? Where will you sit? Is it with your ex or not? What if you or they have a new partner? Do you celebrate together or separately?
    - Do this for every event you can think of, from softball games and piano recitals to weddings and births.
- If you are working Collaboratively with your spouse, do this individually and then compare together or bring it to a team meeting to share.
- Are there important friends and traditions that you can reshape to support your new family? How does this look?

CHAPTER 9 | RESULT

> You're fifteen years in the future. You unexpectedly run into your ex-spouse. You are with one of your closest friends from when you were married. How do you feel? How does your friend feel? How does your ex feel?

Describe your future family here:

- You will have a vision for your future, unique and specific to you and your family, to base the rest of your practical decisions on.

CHAPTER 9 | **HIGHLIGHTS**

- Spending time envisioning far into the future to see what you want your family to look like gives you a road map to make more practical decisions.
- Staying focused on the future can help inform decisions based on what you want for your children and your children's children.
- If you don't share children, doing future-focused exercises can help shape the social connections you'll maintain after you are no longer married.

CHAPTER 10

Building Your Parenting Plan

Thousands of candles can be lighted from a single candle, and the life of the single candle will not be shortened. Happiness never decreases by being shared.
—Paraphrase of Section 10 of the Sutra of 42 Sections, attribution "The Teaching of Buddha"

DIVORCE IS A DIFFICULT TIME for everyone involved, especially children. It's important to remember that as parents, our priority should always be the well-being and happiness of our kids. While it can be easy to get caught up in the emotions and drama of divorce, it's crucial to put aside personal differences and focus on creating a healthy environment for your children.

This chapter highlights how to build a Parenting Plan and what to address. A well-thought-out and comprehensive parenting plan is better for your children and better for you. Predictability helps children adjust to change at every age.[25] When you and your ex can

25 Early Childhood Learning & Knowledge Center. 2020. "The Importance of Schedules and Routines | ECLKC." Eclkc.ohs.acf.hhs.gov. June 1, 2020. https://eclkc.ohs.acf.hhs.gov/about-us/article/importance-schedules-routines.

co-parent on the same page, you're not only gifting your children a better chance at adjusting well, but you are also setting up a framework for you, as parents, to know what to expect from the other. Your kids will know what's happening and what comes next. You will be able to use the roadmap your parenting plan provides to plan your days, when you are "parent on duty" and not.

Often divorce means one parent returns to work. That parent needs the outline of what their responsibilities are going to look like to find a job that works with it. The parent who worked outside of the home will take on new responsibilities if they've not been the one to take kids to soccer or stay home when they're sick. When you put together a good parenting plan, you're planning for these new circumstances in advance. You're making both the post-divorce transition and your long-term future better for your entire family.

There are resources in the tool section that help you go much deeper into this critical project than the scope of this book can address or many state templates require.

GUIDELINES

When building a parenting plan, remember several essential guidelines:

- Put your child's needs first but do it rationally.
    - The most crucial factor in creating a successful parenting plan is meeting your child's needs. A solid plan considers their age, developmental stage, and any special needs they may have. Considering your kiddos is not the same as letting them decide big things!
- If your state requires a parenting class, do that first.

  - You will have to do it anyway, and it can help you create a more thoughtful and comprehensive plan.

- You are the parent.
  - Your children should not be asked for involvement to threaten or undermine the other parent. Neither you nor your spouse should put them in the middle in any way.
  - Something as subtle as "I'd take you for ice cream because you did so well on your spelling test, but you know Daddy doesn't like that. I know. Let's not tell him. It's our secret." That ice cream and comment puts your child in the middle.
- If you and your spouse cannot agree on a parenting plan, the court will appoint a guardian ad litem.
  - They represent your child/children's interests to the court. They can have a significant impact, but enlisting their participation may not mean you get your desired result.
- Be clear and specific:
  - Your parenting plan should be detailed and include specific schedules for custody, visitation, holidays, and vacations. It should also outline how you will make decisions regarding the child's education, healthcare, expenses, and other vital areas.
- Communicate effectively.
  - For the parenting plan to work smoothly, you must communicate effectively with your co-parent. Be respectful and open-minded when discussing your child/ren issues.
- Be flexible.
  - Life can be unpredictable, so building flexibility into your parenting plan is essential. Flexibility could mean having

a backup plan in case of unexpected events or agreeing to adjust schedules as needed.

- Consider mediation
    - If you're having difficulty reaching an agreement with your co-parent, consider working with a mediator who can help facilitate productive discussions and find common ground.
- Review and revise regularly
    - As your child grows and circumstances change, it's essential to review your parenting plan regularly and make necessary revisions. Build a schedule for this into your plan.

SPECIFICS TO ADDRESS IN YOUR PARENTING PLAN

Schedules

This is your parenting time. In it, you will show when the children will be with each parent. Often there are on-off patterns to the schedules. Younger children can benefit from seeing parents more frequently, which results in switching households every few days. Longer stays in each home may better serve older children. These patterns represent the everyday schedules parents will use for parent-on-duty time.

Here are some sample patterns for overnights:

Alternating Weeks

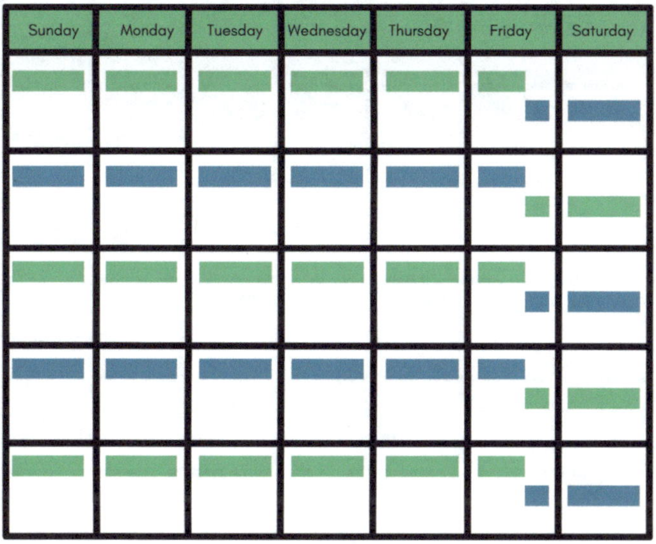

Alternating Weeks with a Mid-Week Visit

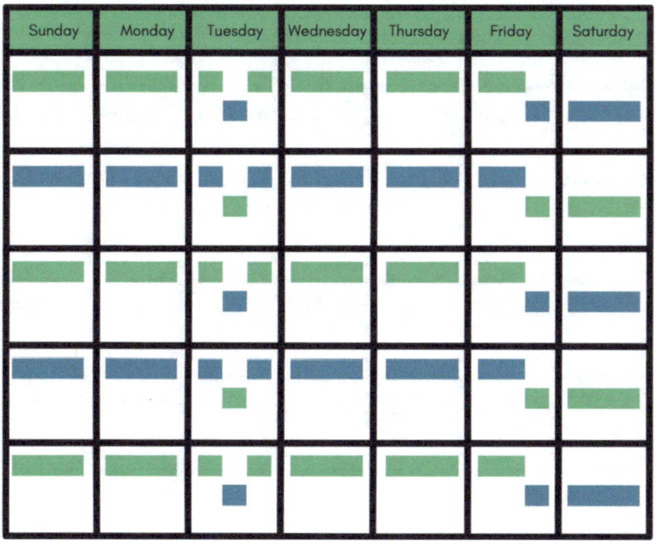

Alternating Weeks with a Mid-Week Overnight

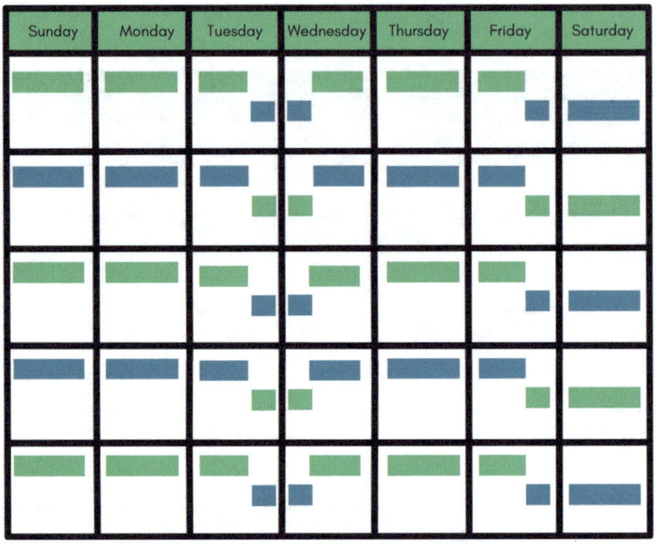

2–2–3

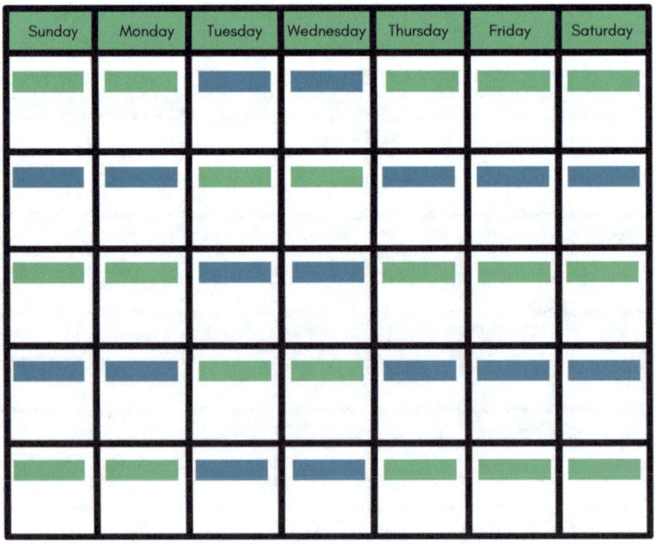

3–3–4–4

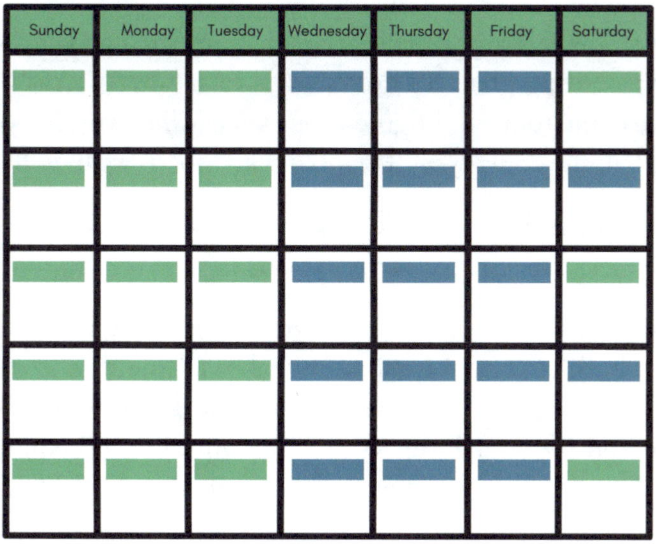
Sunday
Monday
Tuesday
Wednesday
Thursday
Friday
Saturday

2–2–5–5

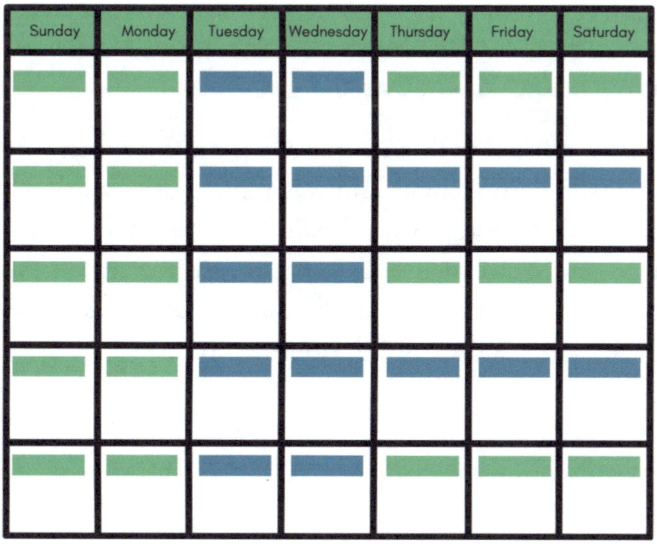
Sunday
Monday
Tuesday
Wednesday
Thursday
Friday
Saturday

Holidays, School, and Special Days

Spell out holidays and other variances from the everyday schedule in your parenting plan. It's not enough to say "we'll cross that road when we come to it" and figure it out later. When you file your parenting plan, the court system wants a plan, not a "we'll do that later."

Often this is done by making a holiday list and designating who has parenting time on even or odd years.

School can have its own challenges if one of the parents ends up with the bulk of school holidays or takes all the days children are sick or have medical appointments off of work. Consider the school calendar and the actual impact on your work life and equity in distribution when you're putting together your Parenting Plan.

Transferring

For regular and holiday schedules, you'll decide what transfers look like between houses. This states who is responsible for getting the kids from one place to another and the timing.

I recently worked with a couple stuck on this topic. The mother had been an at-home parent and was returning to work outside the home. The father thought she should be responsible for getting the children to and from their activities because she always had. Walking through how that would work allowed them to see the logistics through each other's eyes and devise a solution.

Decision-Making

You can decide to make decisions together, or one parent will take some areas, and the other be responsible for different decisions.

Typically, the areas to assign are:

- Education
- Healthcare
- Religion
- Activities

Travel

You will decide what the rules are for your children traveling with one or the other parent. Can they go out of state? What must they communicate to the other parent? Can the other parent deny approval? What is the time frame for prior notice? What are the durations?

Communication

As you build independent households and co-parent your children, it can be handy to devise rules for how you will communicate with each other and how you will communicate with your children during the other's parenting time. Having communication guidelines is often overlooked or deemed a little thing in the overall scheme. It's just those little things that are left untended that can cause an entire agreement to blow up.

Picture this: You're trying to get up to speed in a new job, which is overwhelming. You need to pick the kids up at after-school care before they close, but your new boss gave you a project she wants to be done before you leave. You call your best friend at the last minute to get your kids and spend twenty more minutes finishing your project.

Whew! You can do this.

You glance at your phone when you're dashing to your car to get your kids at the center where your friend's daughter has ballet class. She took them with her because she was late.

There's a text from your spouse. Because you have to hurry to get the kids, you don't read it. While your phone pings again, you grab them from the center, thanking your friend profusely. Ping, another text. But you're late for the boy scout meeting, and the kids haven't eaten yet. You hate feeding them fast food, but it's the only thing you have time to squeeze in.

Now, you're in the drive-through ordering, and your phone rings. Your ex is calling. You're in the middle of the order and can't pick it up. And it feels humiliating that you're picking up fast food; what if he hears? You toss the kids their food, and they eat on the drive to scouts. Once there, your daughter tells you she needs a poster board for her report tomorrow.

You figure you have just enough time to dash to the store with her and return when the meeting ends. There's a train. You're going to be late. You run in; they're out of poster board. The associate is looking in the back when your ex calls again. And again. By the time you pick up your son and get home, you're frazzled, the kids are stressed, and you still haven't read your texts. No time.

Next, supervise the homework. It's after nine by the time you finally pick up your phone to check to see what he needs. You notice there are five voicemails, but read the texts first. It starts with the last one, which says, "If you think you can get away with blocking me out of MY kids' lives, you're going to pay for it." Holy shit, what is that all about? You track back through the text chain, heart beating like you just ran a marathon.

Your spouse had reached out to see how the kids were doing after the first day back to school in the first text, and as hours passed and you didn't answer went from worried to angry to rabid. You ALWAYS answer texts right away. His thinking there must be something wrong has evolved into believing you're blatantly ignoring him!!

Because there weren't communication guidelines in this scenario, something pretty innocent turned into a situation that might derail your parenting plan.

What if this couple agreed to respond to any communication via text once a day before ten pm.? Or agreed that a phone call signaled "this is critical." If it's not urgent = don't call. Could this situation have been avoided? Likely, it would have been easier on both of them. The spouse receiving the calls and texts would have known they had a grace period (or that it was urgent if they got a phone call), and there wouldn't have been additional stress on an already stressful day. The sending spouse probably would have sent one text and waited for the promised response that evening.

When deciding how to communicate, think about what methods are best, what time you'll respond, and when it's OK to share.

Discipline

Often in a household, parents see discipline differently, usually an indication of the punishments they received as a child. One parent might believe in natural consequences, and one might think spankings are the answer. There may also be a huge difference in the view of what is a punishable offense. Infractions can vary wildly, from not "showing respect" (whatever that means) to drug and alcohol use.

There can be a tendency for each parent to think, "Finally, I can do this the way I want to, the way it should have done it all along."

Think about how confusing this can be for kids and how difficult it can be to carry out between households. Talk about the realities of this in your Parenting Plan. What will you do if one parent chooses to discipline a child while it's their parenting time, and the other parent doesn't uphold that? I've seen this cause a lot of anger among parents, ultimately harming the children.

Other Thoughts to Consider

Other ways to prioritize your children during divorce (depending on age and maturity):

- Keep their routines as consistent as possible. This means maintaining regular schedules for meals, bedtime, schoolwork, and extracurricular activities. Children thrive on structure and stability, so having a predictable routine can help ease anxiety.
- Encourage your children's relationship with your ex-spouse. Even if you have negative feelings toward each other, try not to speak negatively in front of your kids.

- They are kids. Even late teens are still children. Don't put them in a position of taking on parental roles that used to be filled by your spouse.

By keeping their best interests at heart and creating a stable environment for them during this challenging time, you can help your children adjust and thrive post-divorce.

> Smiling through difficulty isn't a useful coping skill for kids—but it does send a strong message: If you're not happy, it's because there's something wrong with you, and you don't want other people to find out.
> —Dan Robitzski

CHAPTER 10 | DO THE WORK

- Know the Parenting Plan requirements in your jurisdiction.
- Take any required parenting class as soon as possible.

CHAPTER 10 | RESULT

> "We want what's best for the kids" is a common joint statement. How will you keep that your focus as you and your spouse figure out how to co-parent?

- The best result for a kid with divorced parents is to feel loved and supported by both parents and to have a positive and healthy relationship with each of them.

Write your parenting vision statement here:

CHAPTER 10 | **HIGHLIGHTS**

The Parenting Plan is your roadmap for co-parenting.

- A more thorough, complete parent plan avoids disagreements later.
- Skipping over an area to decide it post-divorce is troublesome.
- Setting communication parameters between parents will avoid misunderstandings that lead to more giant blow-ups.

CHAPTER 11

Dealing with Traditions and Firsts

Every day brings new choices.
—Martha Beck

AS YOU GO THROUGH YOUR DIVORCE AND FOR YEARS AFTER, you'll keep coming up against firsts. The first time you attend a recital without your spouse. Your first wedding anniversary when you're no longer married. You will also face at least a year of firsts for your family traditions. These can be highly emotional events, and planning to get through these times can decrease the negative impact. Approached thoughtfully, you may create even more lovely, bonding, memorable traditions moving forward.

This chapter will discuss how you may look at your traditions and first-time experiences as a single person.

TRADITIONS AND HOLIDAYS

Many of us have special memories associated with certain holidays, anniversaries, or events that we used to celebrate with our former spouse or whole families.

I mentioned my ex's family Christmas party. It's always on Christmas Eve, very festive and highly attended.

I was not included in our first separated Christmas—when we were in the divorce process. The kids went and have gone almost every year since. It's a tradition important to my ex and his family that carries on for our children. The same Christmas, my soon-to-be-ex wanted to come over on Christmas morning and open presents as a family, as we always had. I wasn't emotionally able to wrap my head around that. I declined because I felt it would be too painful for me. I also thought it would be incredibly awkward and inauthentic. It felt forced, like, "Hey, look how well-adjusted this divorcing family is! We can all still spend Christmas together just as we always have." And, the whole truth, it felt terrible that I was explicitly not included in the Christmas Eve festivities but expected to go through Christmas morning as though it was the same as it had been for the last eighteen years.

In my case, the traditions no longer felt the same; it was impossible to continue. I know divorced families who still open presents together on Christmas morning, attend each other's family parties, and even vacation together.

Neither is right nor wrong. The object is to have a plan that works for you and your mental and emotional well-being, considers any children in an age-appropriate way, and thinks things out thoroughly.

It's important to acknowledge these changes and allow yourself time to grieve the loss of what was. At the same time, it can also be an opportunity to create new traditions that reflect your current situation and bring you joy. It's OK to take things one day at a time and adjust as needed—much of navigating this process is trial and error. Ultimately, it's about finding what works for you and your family as you move forward into this new chapter of your life.

What seasons, holidays, or traditions have special meaning for you individually, for your family together, and for your spouse?

Imagine how you'd like to see each event played out. If you've always been a Halloween person, make note that you'd like to create new traditions. If your spouse makes a massive fête of the Fourth of July, maybe let it be known that you respect that and let it continue for him. If your in-laws were also your best friends, consider talking to them about how you may continue to stay in touch and be involved.

One way to approach this is by starting new traditions that reflect your current situation and values. New practices can be as simple as trying out a new recipe, taking a day trip somewhere you've always wanted to go, or gathering with friends for a game night. The possibilities are endless, don't be afraid to get creative!

Another option is to reframe old traditions in a way that feels more authentic and aligned with your current life. For example, if you used to celebrate Christmas with your ex-spouse's family, consider creating your holiday celebration with close friends or extended family members who have supported you through this transition.

What new landmarks are coming up that don't have family traditions already in place?

What are the things you and your ex might participate in together? Will you attend a child's graduation and have a celebratory dinner afterward? Sometimes things that are firsts in the family are easier. It can be an opportunity to figure out "how are we going to do this." For new things, you may focus on the present moment and find ways to celebrate what is still available.

What happens when new significant others are involved?

I've seen traditions get more complicated once one or both parties have a new significant other. For example, you've chosen to continue a tradition together as a family; maybe it's having dinner together on each child's birthday. Now one parent is dating someone seriously. How do you handle the situation? Do you continue as you were, invite the new significant other or create an entirely different practice?

Ultimately, staying open-minded and flexible as you navigate this process is key. I believe it's also important to honor where you are now in your approach, mental health, and mindset. Breaking old traditions and establishing new ones may be the best thing to help you move forward.

FIRSTS

The first year you're living apart, you will also experience a series of firsts that might be disturbing. For others, they can be a grand celebration.

You will have a first birthday, wedding anniversary, every holiday, maybe first date, first time attending a couples' gathering as a single, first time going to church alone; you get the idea. There will be a lot of them.

Try to anticipate what your experience will be as best you can (some are going to sneak up on you). You know it will be a rocky road on your first Valentine's alone. Go back to your support friends, find a Galentine's event (yes, that is a thing), or maybe allow yourself time to grieve by revisiting old Valentines, but limit the time and end that session envisioning new.

Conversely, perhaps it's your first Thanksgiving holiday, and you don't have to make the stuffing how your spouse wants it. You hate stuffing. There will be no stuffing at the Thanksgiving table. You love rice; there will be rice for the first time and all times going forward. Celebrate the f'in rice!

Finding what works best for you may take some trial and error. Know that there are no right or wrong answers here. By staying true to yourself and embracing change, you can create new opportunities for joy and connection after divorce.

Caveat: You may want to co-create these new traditions with your spouse, especially if you have children. Sometimes that isn't possible or healthy. If you're expected to maintain the status quo at the expense of your well-being, or your ability to move forward, you might need to work on keeping boundaries.

If I'd said, "Sure—come over Christmas morning," but my thought bubble for my husband was, "This is going to be torture. I have to act like everything is the same for the sake of you and the kids. Even though you left me, we're in the midst of a needlessly ugly, expensive divorce. And I'll do all the present wrapping, as usual. And make the breakfast casseroles and sweets, as usual. And clean everything up, as usual," it's obvious that would not have been healthy.

CHAPTER 11 | DO THE WORK

- List traditions and holidays that are important to you, your kids, and your spouse.
- Determine what you'd like to keep and imagine what you may create.
- If age-appropriate, ask your children; if productive and healthy, brainstorm with your spouse.

CHAPTER 11 | RESULT

> It's not the big moments that tend to make the most difference in our memories—it's the little ones. The "remember when" we always had a party in the driveway on Halloween? Remember how we had the cranberry sauce right out of the can with the ridges at Thanksgiving?

What are the "remember whens" you want to keep? To make?

- You'll have a roadmap for what traditions you want to keep and where to start new ones.
- You'll have a plan for where you might need support (or celebration) as you face the "firsts" of becoming single again.

CHAPTER 11 | **HIGHLIGHTS**

- Life will change dramatically, impacting family traditions. There may be ones you want to keep or reimagine. There may be a great opportunity to create new traditions.
- Going through firsts can be painful or a celebration. Trying to identify them in advance and make a plan if and when you need support can help.

CHAPTER 12

Family and Friends Toolbox

If you don't know where you are going,
you will probably end up somewhere else.
—Laurence J. Peter

HERE IS A SELECTION of family-centered tools and resources you may find useful as you work through divorce.

This is not an endorsement of any particular application. Different programs will have different costs and features; some are better for expenses, some for calendars, and some can create reports that you may submit to the court. Look for the features that suit your family and your budget best.

CO-PARENTING APPS

These apps can streamline your schedules, shared expenses, and communications.

Schedules   Expenses   Communication

APP	URL	Best for
2Houses	2houses.com	Schedules, Expenses, Communication
amicable	amicable.io/coparenting-app	Schedules, Communication
AppClose	appclose.com	Schedules, Expenses, Communication
CoParenter	coparenter.com	Schedules, Communication
coparently	coparently.com	Schedules, Expenses, Communication
cozi	cozi.com	Schedules
Custody Connection	custodyconnection.com	Schedules
Custody X Change	custodyxchange.com	Schedules

APP	URL	Best for
DComply	dcomply.com	Expenses
FamCal	apps.appxy.com/FamCal	Schedules
Our Family Wizard	ourfamilywizard.com	Schedules, Expenses, Communication
MyMob	mymob.com	Schedules
Parentship	parentship.co	Schedules
Talking Parents	talkingparents.com	Schedules, Expenses, Communication
Time Tree	timetreeapp.com	Schedules
WeParent	weparent.app	Schedules, Expenses, Communication

RESOURCES ABOUT BUILDING YOUR PARENTING PLANS

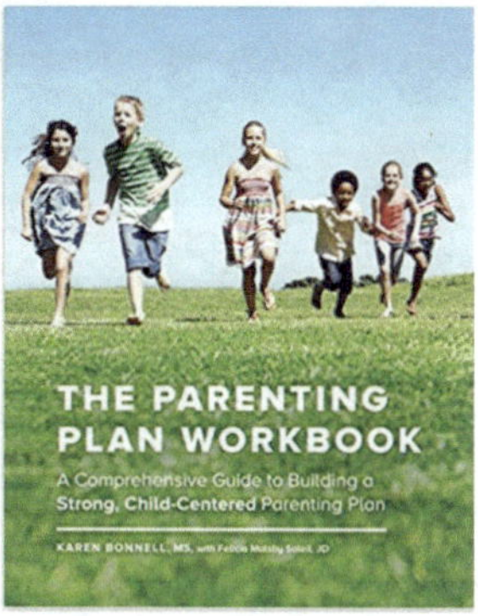

The Parenting Plan Workbook: A Comprehensive Guide to Building a Strong, Child-Centered Parenting Plan

by Karen Bonnell

The Conscious Parent's Guide to Coparenting: A Mindful Approach to Creating a Collaborative, Positive Parenting Plan

by Jenna Flowers

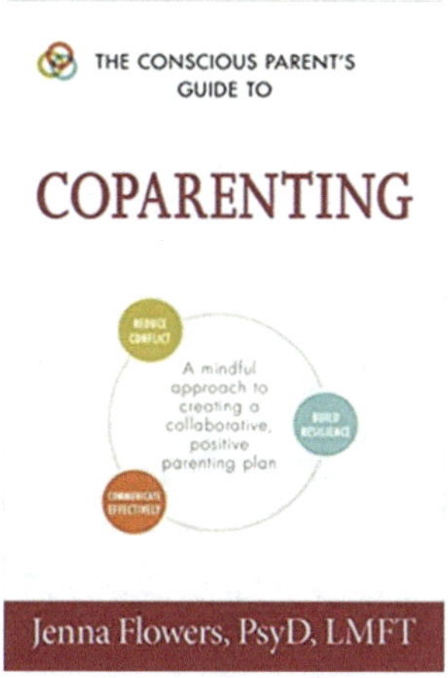

Building a Parenting Agreement That Works: Child Custody Agreements Step by Step Tenth Edition

by Mimi Lee PhD

PART III: FINANCES AND PRACTICAL SHIT

With the right kind of coaching and determination you can accomplish anything.
—Reese Witherspoon

CHAPTER 13

How to Pick Your Professionals

Choose to focus your time, energy and conversation around people who inspire you, support you and help you to grow you into your happiest, strongest, wisest self.

—Karen Salmansohn

IT TAKES A VILLAGE TO GET DIVORCED, AND YOU NEED A TEAM.

This chapter will cover the different professionals you may consider working with, how you find them, what each of them does, and offer some ideas for interviewing them. You can have a much better outcome if you use the right professionals in their expertise *and* save a lot in fees. Also, adding a little bonus for you, some tips on how to use the professionals and manage payments.

WHO DO I NEED ON MY TEAM?

Who you hire to help you through your divorce depends on how complex your situation is and the type of divorce process you plan to use. Think of it as figuring out what you need and finding the right person to help you in that area.

This isn't an exhaustive list, but it gives you an idea of how you can approach building your team. If you find something in the "I need someone who . . ." column that's unique for you, you might need a different professional to help you address that need.

I need someone who helps me…	***Professional***
Understand the rules, explain the legal process, make sure everything is done correctly with the courts, and file or finalize my divorce.	***Family Law Attorney***
Get all of my finances in order, understand my situation - not just through the divorce but after, develop a budget, help evaluate settlement options, avoid mistakes that cost money, decode our retirement plans and benefits - especially when they include things like stock options. Also provide testimony to the court regarding finances, if needed.	***Certified Divorce Financial Analyst®***
Manage the process, think through my options, keep things moving forward, be a thought partner when I run into things that aren't legal or financial in nature.	***Certified Divorce Coach®***

Give us a fact-based accounting of what our business is worth so we can decide how to divide it equitably.	***Business Valuation Specialist***
Figure out what's best for our kids when my soon-to-be ex and I can't come to an agreement, or there's worry about abuse or neglect. This professional is appointed by and reports to the court, not the parents.	***Guardian Ad Litem (GAL)***
Track down money that is (or has been) being hidden or siphoned off our accounts or a business.	***Forensic Accountant***
Won't take sides but will help us come to an agreement when we are stuck.	***Mediator***
Can help me figure out what my skills are and how I can earn money as I move forward on my own. Also who can give a realistic assessment of what I can be earning now, or with additional education or training.	***Vocational Expert***
Help us make decisions for our children regarding the best way to parent together moving forward. This professional works for us, the parents, to help figure out the best options - not the court.	***Child Specialist***

HOW DO I FIND THE RIGHT PARTNERS?

You've either decided to or are considering divorce. As you move through the process, there will be many decisions to make; one of the first, and most important, is the professionals you will have on your team. They have a tremendous impact on the journey and the outcome of your divorce.

Depending on the type of divorce you and your spouse want to pursue, you will need different professionals. This is the first, and I think most important, consideration when you start to put together a divorce team.

You might be limited here if your spouse has already hired an attorney. If their legal counsel is aggressive and known for the high propensity to take cases to court, even if you want to mediate, it might not happen. What your spouse has already done will impact your hiring decisions, too. Remember the saying about bringing a knife to a gunfight?

Let's break down the steps to hiring professionals depending on different scenarios.

Neither you nor your spouse has hired an attorney, mediator, CDC® or CDFA®; you have agreed that you will divorce and have decided on the method you'd like to follow. The process will drive the choice of professionals.

> Couples can pick more than one mediator. They may use a faith-based mediator for their family and CDFA for the financial part.

If you've chosen to mediate, you'll first look for a mediator who practices the type of mediation you'd like to use—transformative, facilitative, or evaluative. You can find mediators in your local Google business listings, on Mediator.com, or through referrals from others who have used that professional. Couples' therapists can also be a resource, particularly if you are looking for someone who practices more in the transformative or facilitative arena. If you belong to a house of faith, especially one that offers couples or individual therapy, they might also be a resource for a mediator who would be appropriate for you.

Divorcing couples can pick more than one mediator. The partners may want to use a faith-based mediator for their family decisions and a CDFA to support them through the financial part of their agreement. This is an excellent example of finding the right person for the task instead of expecting to save money or shortcut the system by using one professional in areas where they are not an expert. In this case, the mediators are working for both of them as neutral parties; they don't represent one or the other.

Visit their website and see if they have any information on social media—blogs, YouTube, a Facebook business page, etc.

If it's available to you, make an appointment to interview them. We offer our clients a complimentary Discovery Call. Suppose they want to dig a little deeper into whether mediation seems to be the proper process for them. In that case, our firm offers a Strategy Session to outline the next steps further, discuss expectations, and answer their questions about the process.

Because a mediator is a neutral position, ensure each spouse has access to the mediator you're considering and their questions have equal weight. Different mediators have different practices and specialties. I usually meet individually with each individual to talk about their vision and goals, as well as any concerns they have, before we have a joint session. This may not be the methodology of the professional you're considering.

This overall outline is appropriate for any professional. Bridging Divorce has also put together a more detailed booklet with questions by profession (CDFA, Certified Divorce Coach, Attorney, and Mediator) which you can download using the link after the questions. Here are some questions and thoughts you may use as you interview.

ESSENTIAL QUESTIONS FOR ALL DIVORCE PROFESSIONALS

- What type of divorce do you practice? (Collaborative, Mediation, Litigation)
- Which do you prefer and why?
- What is most of your experience?
    - *Note:* Are they experienced in the type of divorce you want to pursue? Do they have credentials and training for that? For example, an attorney may say they practice Collaborative law or alternative dispute resolution, but if they are not trained in the Collaborative Divorce Process, it can impact their ability to work productively with a Collaborative team.
- If litigating, what percentage of your cases go to trial? (note: A high rate might indicate a tendency not to negotiate or negotiate effectively.)
- Describe how you work with your clients, both process and style of interaction.
- If I become your client, what expectations should I have regarding how we will communicate? (phone, Zoom, in-person, email)
- What is your typical time frame to respond to your clients?
- Will I be working directly with you or with support staff?

- If support staff (associates, paralegals, other staff) will be involved, to what degree should I expect to work with them versus you?
- What is your fee structure (the professional and any associates)? How will you keep me informed of costs? What costs vs. fees should I expect?
- Is your fee for a trial or travel different from your hourly rate? What is your retainer?
- What do you bill for (specific work), and in what increments?
- How do you interact with other professionals (when applicable)
    - Attorney
    - Financial professionals
    - Divorce coach
    - Child specialist
    - Mediator
- Do you have time to take on my case now?
- Do you know my spouse or their attorney?
- Will associates be working on my case? If so, can I meet them? How would work be divided?
- Who will handle any negotiations on my behalf?
- What input will I have in strategy decisions on my case?
- How do you keep clients informed of any developments? In what time frame?
- Based on what you know of my case, what issues or problems do you foresee?

- Based on what you know of my case, what timing do you think applies?
- Is there ever an occasion when you would talk to or work with my spouse and not me, or the reverse? (for neutrals)
- What resources/software do you use or offer to your clients?
- Do you help us to gather and organize documents?
- What licensing or training do you have?

For a complete brochure with questions arranged by the area of expertise, visit here:

BONUS

Sometimes a professional might be genuinely qualified, and you still may not "click" with them. Here are some additional questions to ask yourself . . .

- Am I comfortable with this person?
- Do I feel like they are straightforward?
- Do I feel as though the professional listened to me?

- Did they address my concerns or questions?
- Were their answers clear? Condescending?
    - Do they explain things in a way I understand?
    - Do they check in to make sure I comprehend or clarify if I don't?
- Was it easy to schedule a meeting time?
- Was the professional on time for our appointment?
- Were we interrupted during our conversation?
- Is the location convenient?
- Was the office organized and clean? (if applicable)

Please note this is for informational purposes only. Ultimately, the choice to hire professionals in your divorce process is up to you. The goal of these questions is to assist in providing a framework for you to evaluate professionals and make your choice(s).

> If you cannot see where you are going,
> ask someone who has been there before.
> —Loren Norris

CHAPTER 13 | DO THE WORK

- After understanding what type of process you want to pursue, interview the professionals you need to engage in making up your team.
- Interview more than one professional, so you know your options—KEEP NOTES! They may all start sounding the same after a while . . .
- Look for clear responses; check them off your list if they don't answer your question or make you feel comfortable.

CHAPTER 13 | RESULTS

> Are you willing to entrust this person or team with guiding you through what can be an emotional and confusing process?

What is important to you in your divorce professionals? (They're out there . . . don't settle.)

- You will know what is most important to you and how to ask the questions to get you the support and information you need.

CHAPTER 13 | **HIGHLIGHTS**

- Different processes require different professionals.
- Only work with those you trust.
- Use professionals who have experience in the field you need support in, whether it's the type of practice (litigation vs. Collaborative Process) or the area (coaching vs. financial).
- Using one professional to do multiple jobs can cost more in the long run, in fees and mistakes.

CHAPTER 14

Get Grounded. How to Look at Finances. AKA Nobody Wins Divorce.

The four most expensive words in the English language are, 'This time it's different.'
—Sir John Templeton

DIVORCE CAN BE A CHALLENGING AND EMOTIONAL EXPERIENCE, and it's easy to get caught up in the drama and lose sight of the practicalities. If you want to come out of the process with your financial future intact, staying grounded and taking a realistic look at your finances is essential.

> It's about making practical decisions while acknowledging the emotions behind them.

It's easy to lose sight of why you're making your decisions. They're new and coming at you fast and furious. In part because there's a lot of emotion involved in your choices. *Especially* the financial ones.

The subtitle of this book is *The Guide to Keeping Your Dignity and Dollars.* It's not about having a bargain divorce or getting the better of your spouse. It's about making practical decisions while acknowledging the emotions behind them.

To own your feelings while making decisions:

- Be honest about your assets, debts, income, and expenses—even if that means facing uncomfortable truths.
    - Trying to hide things is seldom successful and often costs much more than disclosing them in the first place.
- Get clear on your financial goals.
    - You did much work on what you want life to look like in Part 1, *Frame of Mind.* Revisit this. Are your financial goals congruent with that? Do they support it?
- Dig into <u>why</u> you want what you want in your settlement. What is your motivation?
    - Revenge? Fear? Stability? Others' opinions?
- Don't think you can circumvent the rules in your jurisdiction. They're there for a reason and provide the framework for your settlement.
    - Does saying you won't pay spousal support when the laws in your state clearly state you should make you feel better? Ultimately, you'll probably pay more in legal fees trying to fight it and still end up paying support anyway.

Remember that nobody wins in a divorce. With a qualified attorney and divorce financial advisor, you can work toward both of you moving forward stably, sustainably, and as whole as possible.

They can help you navigate the complexities of divorce finance, including issues such as spousal support, child support payments, property division, and tax implications. Staying focused on the practicalities of the situation and approaching it with clarity and honesty will better equip you to emerge from this difficult time with your dignity intact and your financial future secure.

CHAPTER 14 | DO THE WORK

- Go back to your "why" from the first section, "Frame of Mind." Has it shifted?
- Stay grounded in the life you want moving forward; move toward that. Match all of the financial decisions you are facing to that. Are they moving you closer to the life you want or farther away?
- For every decision, examine your motivation. Is it equitable? Is it grounded in reality? Or is it winning or revenge?

CHAPTER 14 | RESULTS

> How much is it worth to you in time, dollars, and emotional capital to approach your process with dignity and equity vs. trying to "win"?

- Clarity and full disclosure about finances ultimately save you money.
- There are not many "tricks" to outsmart the system or your spouse. Overcomplicating or hiding things benefits attorneys and other professionals. Not you, your spouse, or your kids.
- Be prepared for tough conversations grounded in reality, not wishes.

CHAPTER 14 | **HIGHLIGHTS**

- Keep revisiting your motivation behind the financial decisions.
- Don't try to hide the money; it costs more in the end.
- Attempting to evade the system to get more or pay less is time-consuming and expensive.

CHAPTER 15

Understanding Child and Spousal Support

Economics is everywhere, and understanding economics can help you make better decisions and lead a happier life.
—Tyler Cowen

MISCONCEPTION OFTEN DILUTES the best-case scenario when it comes to divorce. There are misconceptions about what financial support post-divorce is, what it is supposed to do, and its foundation. These things have the potential to lead to considerable disagreements as you go through your divorce process, making you deviate from what could be.

Knowing what to expect and, as importantly, what not to expect will significantly impact your settlement process.

There's a lot of emotion attached to support, no matter what we name it or how we categorize it. Some labels carry more baggage than others. There are two primary types of support: spousal support and child support. Depending on where you live, spousal support may be called alimony or spousal maintenance.

Let's start with defining each type of support you could encounter so you can identify what applies to your situation. Remember, each state and potentially different jurisdictions within that state has its own set of rules. You'll need to know what applies to you where you live. It can be entirely unlike another family, only miles away.

Working with a CDFA in putting together your settlement makes it much more likely you will deal with all the financial issues you should while going through your divorce. Revisiting them later is almost always much more costly.

CHILD SUPPORT

If you have children, child support will address the question of financial support for the kids.

Figuring out the amount continues to move toward being determined by a formula in all states. Several different models are used to calculate child support across the country.

The state where you reside determines the formula used in your divorce case (or the state where your children live if it's different).

Some of the standard models used to calculate child support include:

1. The Income Shares Model: *This model, used in most states, calculates child support based on the combined income of both parents. The theory behind this model is that children should receive the same proportion of parental income after divorce as they would have if the parents had remained together.*

2. The Percentage of Income Model: *A few states use this model to calculate child support. Under this model, child support is a set percentage of the non-custodial parent's income.*

3. The Melson Formula: *Used in a few states, this model calculates child support based on the needs of the child and the resources of each parent. Support is then determined by looking at each parent's ability to pay and how much time each parent spends with the child*

Judges can use discretion to deviate from the formula for their state to account for unique circumstances. For example, a judge may order a higher child support payment if one parent earns a significantly higher income than the other, the child's standard of living would be adversely affected from what it was pre-divorce, and it's affordable for the payee.

The basic formulas are usually relatively simple, though many additional factors can influence the final amount.

While that may seem black and white, especially compared to spousal support, it can get cloudy when parents interpret what child support covers and the amounts used to feed into the calculation to arrive at a number.

So, while there is a formula, what you put into the equation will significantly affect your output.

Let's look at some examples:

Billie and Stan live in a state that uses the income shares model, but they make more money combined than the law in their state accounts. Billie, who has her own business, contends that her income is what she pays herself in salary. Stan earns about 20 percent of what Billie brings home and will continue to take on most of the parenting responsibilities for their two children in their agreement. He also knows that Billie is keeping significant funds in her business as capital and running a lot of her personal expenses through the company, making her income look lower.

- Based on Billie's reported income of $240,000 per year and 120 overnights, and Stan's of $56,000, **Billie will pay Stan child support of $1,591 per month**.
- If Billie is actually bringing in $450,000, as Stan guesses, the monthly **child support amount is $2,564**.

Child support is meant to cover that parent's contribution for food, shelter, and clothing. The reason to have child support is to minimize the impact of the divorce on the children's standard of living. You can see how this would happen if two households had vastly different incomes. Changing standards of living happen all the time. Suppose one parent was a stay-at-home caregiver, not working outside the home for many years. The likelihood of that parent returning to a paying job and earning similar to the established spouse is low. So how are other expenses paid on behalf of the child?

> One of the areas you should address is how all the things outside of food, shelter, and clothing will be handled.

As you evaluate your divorce settlement discussions, discuss who will pay for everything outside of food, shelter, and clothing. This can range from extracurricular activities to college applications and class trips to sports uniforms.

Sometimes parents will agree to split these costs evenly. Other times, each will pay according to their percentage of income.

So, if Eric earns 70 percent of their total earnings and James earns 30 percent, Eric pays for 70 percent of their son's violin lessons, while James covers 30 percent. Parents must also agree on how they will decide what their children participate in and who has ultimate decision-making power if there isn't agreement.

Sometimes people will also write about how they will reach an agreement, for example, returning to mediation, if they find themselves at an impasse.

Try to be as forward thinking and comprehensive as possible when you complete your settlement. It can save a lot of expenses and potentially damaging arguments down the road.

Frequently, parents will build into their agreements the method and frequency they will use to settle expenses. Some talk weekly or monthly and transfer funds back and forth as stated in their contract. Others might fund an account for all the estimated children's expenses for the year, each drawing from that as needed.

Not having a clear outline of what expenses are OK and what are not can lead to one parent having to cover a much more significant share of costs than the other.

A prime example of this is automobile expenses for teenagers. A couple of teen drivers in a household can drive insurance costs up quickly. And if your teen gets in an accident, how will those costs be covered? I've seen these expenses run into tens of thousands of dollars. When the settlement does not address them, one parent may pay without help from the other.

Bottom line, do your absolute best to lay out all scenarios in your settlement agreement because times will change, life will go on, and opinions and interpretations can shift. The more details you can lay out in the beginning—making your family road map for decisions and finances—the better you'll be and less likely to end up fighting with each other or through the court system.

Some expenses that can impact child support paid

Health care premiums

Distribution of overnights at parents' homes

Private schooling

Disabilities

Job loss

Extenuating circumstances

Other vital things to know about child support—courts do not want to waive it. It's there to protect the safety and well-being of the child. Parents may declare they are not paying for it, don't need it, or want it. The Family Law system does not want people taking that into their own hands. If there are child support guidelines in your state, and most likely there are, you are going to pay or receive child support according to that formula.[26]

Sometimes payers will get the idea that by reducing or eliminating their income, they will get out of paying child support. Judges are wise; they see through this and don't look kindly on parents trying to shirk their responsibility of providing for their children and might impute income (attribute to them what they could be earning) to the person who is supposed to be paying.[27]

26 *Child support laws and expectations - US news & world report.* (n.d.). Retrieved March 24, 2023, from https://money.usnews.com/money/personal-finance/family-finance/articles/child-support-laws-and-expectations.

27 Deckard, Mallory. 2017. "Child Support and Deliberate Reduction of Income: What Can You Do?" Kahn, Dees, Donovan & Kahn, LLP. July 10, 2017. https://kddk.com/2017/07/10/child-support-and-deliberate-reduction-of-income-what-can-you-do/.

Child support can be a complex and sensitive issue. When you start the process, learn the rules your state uses and their enforcement.

SPOUSAL SUPPORT

> If you find yourself in the position I was, know this:
> your contribution was and remains very worthwhile.
> If your former partner doesn't see it, that's on them.

If child support can be touchy, spousal support can be a ticking bomb. There are cases I've worked on where the higher-earning spouse believes they should, as a matter of duty or promise, help support the lower-earning spouse. These spouses recognize that the support of the at-home spouse helped build their ability to be high-income earners.

More often, it's a point of contention.

I never thought I'd be in a position to start a new career at fifty, after being out of the professional world for years, because I was raising a family and doing all the at-home things. And there I was, here I am. My spouse did not want to pay spousal support and belittled me for not contributing to our income over the years. In the heat of my divorce, there was apparent amnesia regarding the years I earned outside our home. In addition to being a mom, wife, and supporter in our community, I made a significant amount for many years. It was a big pill for me to swallow when the person I thought I was supporting in his career trajectory (while doing all the other things) told me my contribution was worthless.

If you find yourself in the position I was, know this: **your contribution was and remains worthwhile**. If your former partner doesn't see it, that's on them.

HOW SPOUSAL SUPPORT WORKS

There are generally three types of spousal support that may be awarded during divorce proceedings:

1. Temporary
2. Rehabilitative
3. Permanent.

People may also receive a lump sum instead of a series of alimony payments.

Temporary (or short-term) spousal support is typically granted during the divorce process to help the lower-earning spouse meet their financial needs while the legal proceedings are ongoing. This type of support is meant to be a short-term solution until a more permanent arrangement can be made.

Rehabilitative spousal support is awarded when one spouse requires financial assistance to obtain education or training that will enable them to become self-supporting. This type of support is often given for a fixed period and may be contingent upon the recipient meeting specific requirements, such as completing a degree program or obtaining a certain level of employment.

Permanent (or long-term) spousal support is less common than temporary or rehabilitative support. Some states have set formulas based on income and the duration of the marriage, while others are more arbitrary and decided by a judge based on similar cases. It is often awarded in cases where one spouse has been out of the workforce for an extended time or has limited earning potential due to factors such as age, health, or disability. In these situations, the court may order ongoing financial assistance from one spouse to the other indefinitely.

When working with clients in states that don't have specific formulas to determine spousal support, we try to approach it with a needs-based method. What will it cost the recipient to live separately? Is there enough income to support the recipient spouse as they reenter the workforce or get additional training?

Check the guidelines in your state to see how spousal support is handled. Common misconceptions are that a spouse will receive long-term payments after a short-term marriage. It can happen, but it is rare.

Here are examples of what spousal support may look like in different areas (based on the couple, Mary and Mark, used in the Appendix). The first shows what may happen in Illinois, where there is a guideline formula. The second is Tennessee, where there isn't a guideline. The third shows how a needs-based analysis can come up with an in-between figure that leaves both parties meeting their needs.

- In Illinois, Mark would pay Mary $4,770.58 per month for 14 years and 3 months.
- In Tennessee, there is no formula. Mary may receive some alimony for a few years as rehabilitative payments (so she has time to get on her feet and earn her own way). We don't know what this number is or how long it would be paid.
- In a Collaborative case with the same facts, the support may be determined to be need-based. Figuring that Mary needs additional training, which will cost $18,000 to make the income that will meet her needs, she may receive a lump sum of $18,000 for a training program and $6,789 per month for 5 years. This will cover her expenses while she completes training and allow her to meet her share of the income needs after five years.

PLACES WHERE SPOUSAL SUPPORT CAN GET TRICKY

These are some ways determining spousal support can get thorny, even in states with a formula. If you find yourself in one of these situations, enlist the services of a CDFA to help navigate figuring out support:

- One or both of you own a business
- You have a business that can be treated as both an asset(s) and income
- One or both of you is in partnership with another individual
- Long-term marriage with one working spouse
- Personal expenses are paid by a business
- Income includes stock grants
- Bonus or commission makes up a portion of income

It's important to note that spousal support laws vary by state and jurisdiction, so it's always best to consult with a qualified attorney who can help you understand your specific rights and obligations related to spousal support.

CHAPTER 15 | DO THE WORK

- Learn the child support and spousal support guidelines at use in your state.
- Get clear on what is considered income.
- Figure out your expenses or a budget when you are living separately. (I use several software programs to help my clients do this, dTour.life and eMoney are two of them.)
    - Here's a spreadsheet you can download to pull together your expenses.
    - Remember that these are your estimated post-divorce expenses, not what you spent while married.
- Do you require additional training or education to support yourself? What would that look like?

CHAPTER 15 | RESULTS

If you don't understand what it takes to live independently, how will you assess your settlement?

- You will have a realistic expectation of what you will get or pay in spousal support based on your state guidelines (if they exist).
- You will know how to approach spousal support if you live in a state that does not use a formula.

CHAPTER 15 | **HIGHLIGHTS**

- Child support is determined by a formula and intended to be spent for the child's food, shelter, and clothing.
- Other types of children's expenses, such as extracurricular activities, should be considered in your agreement.
- Spousal support may be determined by a formula where you live; it may not.
- Develop a budget for after divorce so you know if you can live on any settlement being discussed or if you can afford to live on what remains if you are the payor.
- Get help with anything you have questions about.

CHAPTER 16

What You Spend

Money, like emotions, is something you must control to keep your life on the right track.
—Natasha Munson

YOUR EXPENSES ARE ALSO commonly called your budget. I avoid the latter because most people think of *budget* as a dirty word. My more critical reason for avoiding it is that it stands more for scarcity than abundance. When people think of a budget, it conjures up the same baggage as *diet*, with visions of doing less and having less.

Many people, when faced with putting together their expenses for a financial affidavit, scale way, way back from their usual standard of living. In my practice I find this happens most frequently with women. Divorce may plant the notion that leads to an *I can do without that* mindset **before** any work has been done or discussions are had. It is not your job to start the divorce process from the point of sacrifice. There may, and likely will, come a time when it is necessary. You are, after all, taking one household and splitting it into two with the same amount of money coming in (at least at first) as you had with one home.

You're not there yet.

By giving your expenses a haircut before you've got a complete picture of all your finances, you're not helping anyone. It may seem like you are being helpful by being frugal and giving. You're beginning the conversation by saying, "I can do with less," and it's nearly impossible to go back to needing more when you already said you could get by with less.

Here's the worksheet from Chapter 15 to prompt you to think about what you spend.

Remember, when filling out your expenses, consider things you may pay annually, not monthly, like car and home insurance. These yearly amounts can be divided by twelve to get to your monthly figure. You may also have to do homework for estimates of expenses that will change as you move into independent living. Costs shared among family members, like cell phones, health insurance, and even Netflix, will likely increase when they are not part of a group plan.

Beyond those typical expenses, it can be more work to separate children's expenses. Even so, budgeting children's expenses clarifies what you are spending on your own and what portion of expenses go directly to the kids. It also helps to demonstrate the additional need for children's expenses beyond food, shelter, and clothing. Beyond the driving costs, as mentioned earlier, some costs that can add up for children are extracurricular activities and lessons, tutors, college prep tests, exams, and applications. Your kids will be unique and change as they grow. Accounting for these "extras" as best you can, produces a more realistic projection of family expenses.

You can also use tracking apps like Mint. I provide my clients one of two portals—dTour.life is specific to divorce and can connect directly to your accounts or be populated manually. I also offer eMoney® websites where clients can plan, link their investments and credit cards, and get a clear and ongoing picture of their spending.

CHAPTER 16 | DO THE WORK

- Track your expenses for a reasonable projection.
  - Prior expenses can demonstrate the standard of living the family was used to experiencing.
  - Current expenses help point out where costs will change with two households and make both parties aware of costs they might not have managed.
  - Future projections will help you map income and lifestyle post-divorce.

(A CDFA® can help you look years into the future to see if what you anticipate spending is viable or if you'll run out of funds and when.)

- Bonus: Try dividing your expenses into categories.
  - Those you absolutely need—food, shelter, clothing.
  - Those that add to your quality of life or are meaningful to you—gym membership, lessons, dining out, etc.
  - Those that are indulgences—luxury travel, first class, five-star restaurants, etc.
  - Total each of these. You may have been too frugal if basic needs are the majority (or all) of your budget. If your indulgent total is the more significant percentage of expenditures, you could reasonably be expected to pare back.

CHAPTER 16 | RESULTS

Do you know what you spend? When you don't know what's going out, it's near impossible to make good decisions on a day-to-day basis, and much more likely, you will make financial mistakes that both could have been avoided and may not be quickly recovered from.

- When you know what you are spending and what you spend it on, you have a roadmap for good decisions.
- You will have the ability to know what essential expenses are—like a place to live; and what discretionary expenses are—like another pair of shoes in an already crowded closet.
- You can assess the numbers you're working with in settlement discussions based on what it will take to have a decent standard of living.

CHAPTER 16 | **HIGHLIGHTS**

- Tracking your expenses can be educational, particularly if you are not the manager of the money in your household.
- Projecting your spending in the future gives you guidelines to make decisions about what you buy and what you need to live on.
- If your expenses exceed your income, the sooner you address it, the better.

CHAPTER 17

What You Earn

Money is only a tool. It will take you wherever you wish, but it will not replace you as the driver.
—Ayn Rand

WE'RE LOOKING AT INCOME from two angles when working through a divorce.

1. Both incomes are used to determine how much support is paid. Under this lens, people often try to minimize their income because it reduces what they pay.

2. Income is evaluated to see if it's sufficient to support a decent standard of living. This is mapped against expenses to see if there is enough, too much, or too little.

You may be asking how there could possibly be too much. Picture a situation where one person in the divorce, for whatever reason, just wants to get it done and move on. In this case, they may agree to pay more than the other spouse needs. Not every day, but it does occur. When the person "overpays," they provide support income far beyond the other party's needs, as shown by their spending before divorce and their projections. In this case, the person paying may end up living a sparse existence to keep this commitment to a higher-than-average level of support.

INCOME FROM THE LEGAL PERSPECTIVE

Defining income is essential to divorce legal proceedings and child support determinations.

Income refers to the money that a person earns from all sources—including wages, salaries, tips, bonuses, commissions, rental income, investment earnings, and any other form of compensation. In some cases, non-monetary benefits such as health insurance or the use of a company car may also be considered part of a person's income.

- When someone owns their own business, some personal expenses might be run through it and artificially deflate what an individual earns. These amounts are compensation and should be added to the earner's total.
- When someone receives executive compensation that doesn't show on a paystub, like stock grants or shares in a business, these can also be considered income and used in support calculations.

When determining income for legal purposes, it's essential to consider all revenue sources to accurately represent a person's financial situation. This can help ensure fair and equitable decisions regarding spousal support, child support payments, and property division.

Even in states with formulas for determining support using income, sometimes the earnings of one or both parties are off the scale. This may be another good time to engage a Certified Divorce Financial Analyst, otherwise known as a CDFA®, and look at needs beyond the formula. This is the optimal path, otherwise, the situation will resort in court battles that can leave both parties with less (and professionals with more) in the long run.

INCOME FROM A BUDGETING PERSPECTIVE

Long-term financial requirements are often overlooked in divorce. Consider Cathy's story.

Cathy came to me after working with an attorney on her divorce proceedings for several months. She kept asking her lawyer questions about how the process worked, what she could expect, and what to do. The answer she got each time was that she needed to trust her attorney and stop asking questions. And then, each time, she was billed for that answer in increments of six minutes.

Feeling extremely uncomfortable and unsupported, Cathy found me after hearing me on a podcast talking about understanding the finances of your agreement. At our first meeting, she shared that Cathy thought she would be OK because their shared assets were about $800,000, and she expected to receive half of that. Most of it being from the equity in their house. It's important to know that Cathy was not working outside of the home and hadn't during her entire nineteen-year marriage. She homeschooled their kids, and it was something they both agreed on doing when the kids were younger. They were both on the same page about this, all up until he asked for a divorce.

Cathy and I talked about her going to work and what she could expect to earn, about understanding what they spent to keep the house running, and what school would cost if she worked outside of the home instead of home-schooling. We worked together over a couple of sessions to come up with a budget that showed annual expenses to keep the house would be about $80,000, and that was if her husband agreed to pay the tuition for a private school because the public schools where they lived weren't considered good or safe.

As we worked through the process, Cathy could see that $80,000 in cost meant more like $100,000 in income because of taxes. And that if only $100,000 of her expected share of assets was accessible (remember liquidity?), she would only have about a year of expenses before she would need to sell the house or earn $100,000 a year. Since her husband left, she'd worked at a minimum-wage retail position for about $11 an hour. The numbers didn't add up. At least they didn't add up in her favor.

Cathy showed up at a mediation understanding her financial position, goals, and bottom line. Because of this, when her attorney suggested she agree to the proposal for LESS THAN half the marital assets and no spousal support of any kind, she could say no, with cause. And she released that lawyer and hired another attorney who respected her right to ask questions and have them answered.

Having first done the spending exercises in Chapter 16, you now understand the funds you need coming in to live. You know that taxes will impact that in some cases, like earned income, and not in others, like support payments. These used to be taxable to the recipient and deductible by the payor; that law changed for divorces that became final after January 1, 2019.[28]

As you go through this, also understand that income may change between parties over time. Even after your divorce is final, it may serve as a basis to modify your legal agreement.

One last note to beware of, if your settlement uses confusing or unclear language as to what allows modification or what counts as income, you may end up back in court. These arguments can be costly from a legal fee perspective. It may cost even more if the language allows the payee spouse to not hold up their end of the agreement because of a legal loophole or interpretation.

28 "Topic No. 452 Alimony and Separate Maintenance | Internal Revenue Service." n.d. www.irs.gov. https://www.irs.gov/taxtopics/tc452.

CHAPTER 17 | DO THE WORK

- What are your income sources? Are they reliable, and is there room for growth?
- Do you need time to increase your income to a living wage? Do you need additional training or education?
- Consider a vocational assessment if you need help assigning a number to your earning potential or determining what career(s) your skills may qualify you for.

CHAPTER 17 | RESULTS

> How can you hit the target if you don't know what it is?

- You'll know your current income and whether there are gaps in income and expenses.
- You'll understand if you need to work outside the home if you don't already, and what you need to earn.
- You'll be able to see if adjustments are needed in expenses to come to a viable settlement.

CHAPTER 17 | **HIGHLIGHTS**

- Income is essential to determine child and spousal support.
- Earned income from a job isn't the only income counted—many sources exist.
- Mapping actual income against your expenses gives you information to decide whether you can live with a settlement agreement, either as the recipient or payor, or if other things need to change.

CHAPTER 18

About Separating Assets and Liabilities in Divorce

Know what you own, and know why you own it.
—Peter Lynch

YOU SPEND MUCH OF YOUR MARRIED LIFE acquiring assets, and each one of those assets comes with emotional attachments. Our first house was an absolute catastrophe when we bought it. I mean, cockroaches couldn't get out of there fast enough. It took us five years of essentially DIY renovation while we juggled our day jobs.

We laughed and cried (and yelled a bit) through late-night, trial-and-error manual labor. I remember stripping old painted radiators with chemicals and a blowtorch. Don't try that. I'm lucky I didn't burn the house down. There was the struggle to get a cast iron bathtub out of the second floor (again, lucky no one was crushed by a five-hundred-pound bathtub bouncing down the stairs). Over the years, that run-down old cottage became a home with many rich memories.

As you move out of married life and onto your respective futures, you'll likely have poignant memories that will influence how you and your soon-to-be ex split up assets. Remember that you will both have things you are attached to, probably for various reasons. Our emotional attachment to things can color the actual value of that "thing." Remember, it's only stuff, and you may be better off if you can keep a perspective on its monetary value instead of its emotional significance. As always, I'm not trying to tell you what to do, but reminding you to be mindful of your decisions and the influence your emotions can have on them. You may decide you're willing to fight to the bitter end for possession of your old sofa; I ask that you clarify *why* you're fighting for it. Is it the sofa, or is it the "win?"

I recently worked with a client who had great clarity on her *why*. Her husband had cheated on her and lied about it for years. When we were talking about her options in the settlement, her goal (at the time) was not to make sure she had adequate money to live and support her two children. Her goal was to get revenge for all the hurt he caused her over the years and cause him the same shame, embarrassment, and pain he had inflicted on her.

We discussed that if she ruined him to the point where he would no longer have a job or be able to get one, he wouldn't be able to support the kids. She considered this and didn't care. She was immensely clear-headed about her purpose. While not one I endorse, it's not mine to judge. Divorce can take an extremely long time, and her position may shift as she moves through it. Maybe it won't. She makes informed decisions and is unambiguous about what she wants and the repercussions of getting that. Every story isn't rainbows and unicorns. In my view, that's alright. Having gone through what she did for years, she may feel that this is what she needs to heal right now. In a few months, with space and support, she may (or may not) feel differently.

That being said, let's get to it and talk about assets and liabilities.

It's important to consider all your options and understand the implications of each before making any decisions, so I will break it down in several ways.

First, we need to understand what "assets" are. According to Investopedia, an asset is a resource with economic value that an individual, corporation, or country owns or controls with the expectation that it will provide a future benefit. Assets are usually listed on a balance sheet and include cash, investments, property, and equipment.

I'll simplify that. Your assets are your stuff. But the value of your assets is only what someone else will pay for them. Read that again. Understanding your assets is essential. They can be used to generate income or wealth. And mistakes made through errors or misunderstandings can mess you up financially.

> When you don't know what you're looking for or understand what you're agreeing to,
> It's time to call in a CDFA®.

I can't count the times I've spoken to someone about my work and heard, "I wish I knew you when I got a divorce. I made so many mistakes." Or, "I should have been in good financial shape for life. Instead, I'm working for minimum wage because I spent all my savings, and it's the only job I've been able to find."

We're here to stop that from happening. And you're reading this, so you've got a big leg up on identifying what makes sense to you and where you might have questions or need some help. Give yourself a giant pat on the back for that.

Below is a list of asset types, followed by questions to consider asking for every asset.

Assets can be:

- Cash
- Investments, like mutual funds, stocks, bonds, annuities, and life insurance that has a cash value
- Real estate—your residence, vacation homes, rental property, land
- Timeshares
- Vehicles—cars, boats, motorcycles
- Art, collectibles, jewelry

Next, who does the asset belong to? Is it mine, my spouse's, or joint?

People often make the mistake of thinking that it's not theirs if it doesn't have their name on it. That is not the case. More likely than not, if acquired during the marriage, it's considered joint (often called "marital") property. This applies to almost everything. You have a business that was started during the marriage—joint property. Your spouse bought a boat after moving into his apartment—marital property.

Some explicit rules exclude property or assets from being considered as jointly owned in the marriage. The two cases in which things acquired while you're married aren't joint—inheritance and gifts. Those are individual. Unless they are shared by using it to purchase something together, then it's considered a gift to the marriage.

Diana and Bob were getting married. Although Bob already owned a house, they wanted to choose one together to start their new life. And they found it, their dream home. But they didn't have enough money for their down payment, so Diana cashed out her 401k and used that.

Because her 401k was earned before they were married, all of that money was premarital, and had she kept it in her separate retirement account when they divorced ten years later, it would have remained hers. Since she used it for the house titled in both names, it was considered a gift to the marriage. She now had to split what had been her life savings with Bob. Salt in the wound—she also had to pay the taxes and penalties on the 401k money since she was under 59 1/2 and single when she withdrew it. Bob's house? He had rented it all those years and never put Diane's name on the mortgage or deed, so it was separate premarital property.

The difference here—Diane's separate property became joint property because she put it into an asset that had both of their names on it. It would have been the same if she had put it in a joint savings account. If you have an inheritance, gift, or premarital asset and you keep it in your own name, it's separate (like Bob's house). If you put it in both of your names and then want to get it back or be compensated for it in case of divorce, that's when trouble starts.

As you're figuring out how to divide things from ours to yours and mine—ask, "Is it liquid?"

Liquid refers to how quickly it can be converted to cash. Why is this important? Liquidity is significant because it lets you quickly convert your asset into cash if needed. This is critical because it means you can access the funds you need when you need them without having to wait or worry about whether or not you'll be able to get your hands on the money.

For something to be considered a liquid asset, it must be convertible into cash relatively quickly and without incurring too much cost. For example, stocks and bonds are typically liquid assets because they can be sold relatively quickly, and it doesn't cost a lot to sell. Other liquid assets include cash, checking accounts, and short-term investments, like certificates of deposit (CDs).

On the other hand, assets that are not considered liquid typically take longer to sell and may be sold at a discount. Think "fire sale." For example, real estate or collectibles are often not considered liquid assets because it can take a long time to find a buyer willing to pay the total value of the asset.

Additionally, these assets may need to be sold at a lower price to attract buyers. If you find yourself where you need access to funds and all your investments are tied up in things that aren't easy to sell, you may lose money by lowering your price to get your funds.

Nancy came to me midway through her divorce process. She had so many questions about her finances, and they were brushed aside by her attorney. Even some of her friends made her feel small when Nancy spoke up about her worries. Nancy had confided to her best friend that it appeared she would get the house in her settlement, free and clear. The retirement accounts and their bank accounts were going to her ex. Nancy's bestie, Sue, was a little jealous. The home was valued at over $600,000 and had no mortgage. Sue told Nancy she'd be set for life with $600,000 and a fresh start.

Nancy was right to be concerned.

You can live in your house. You can't buy groceries with it, or clothing, or pay other bills. And maintaining a place costs money. There are utilities and taxes to pay, and as any homeowner knows, things tend to break down and go wrong. You will need to maintain your asset.

Having liquid assets on hand in case of an emergency or unexpected expense is essential. This way, you can access the cash you need without worrying about selling off your belongings or incurring debt. Consider the liquidity of an asset before completing your financial settlement. You may have a lot, but will you be able to access it and live on it without paying harsh penalties.

In Nancy's example, she would have a valuable asset but no cash flow to keep it up and no income after divorce. She would have been forced to sell it for enough cash to survive. Or potentially find somewhere else to live and rent her home to generate cash flow.

I have my list of assets, and I understand the concept of liquidity. What now?

There are many distinct types of assets, but some of the most common are cash, stocks and bonds, real estate, and vehicles. Each type of asset has its own unique characteristics and risks. Your next task is to determine how accessible each asset is, so you can figure out what makes sense in your settlement.

If you have a significant amount, but you can't access any of it without paying penalties, is that really going to serve you? Or if you have things of value you want to keep, but you are not going to have enough money to keep them up and end up selling them, is that working for you the way you intended?

TYPES OF ASSETS AND HOW "LIQUID" THEY ARE

Cash is the most liquid asset. If you have cash in hand, it's already there and you can use it as you need it. However, cash has no return potential. It's not going to earn you anything. As I write this, we're in the highest inflation position we've experienced in forty years, so cash money is losing value daily.

Stocks and bonds are accessible. You can convert them to cash in a few days. But they can still fluctuate in value and are subject to market conditions. This can make a difference if you need to access funds while the market is down. You could be losing your holdings by not being able to wait until the market value comes back up.

Real estate is a more illiquid asset. This is important to realize, as in Nancy's case, it's often a person's biggest asset. It takes longer to sell and may not sell for its estimated value, depending on what's going on in the market around you. While real estate can appreciate over time, you need to weigh if you can afford to keep it and if you may be put in a position to sell it when conditions are unfavorable.

Luckily, Nancy sought help because she wasn't confident in the settlement situation being presented to her. Once she realized she couldn't maintain or get money from her asset, the house, she returned to the drawing board on their settlement. This time she had her goals front and center, instead of only balancing dollars in columns on a spreadsheet.

Vehicles are another asset. They can also lose value quickly if not well-maintained. They also come with expenses subject to taxes, registration, and insurance costs. Often the clients I work with take the vehicles off the table; each person keeps the car that is theirs. If a title needs to be transferred, they do so, and the person driving the vehicle assumes whatever loan is associated with it. This is because the automobiles (unless they are multiple or collectible) are not going to be sold or split, and their worth is frequently deemed not worth trying to equalize.

The best way to weigh the impact of the asset types on your settlement and cash flow is to consult with a financial advisor educated in the economic situations in divorce, a CDFA®. They can walk you through your expenses, the realities of what you'll need to meet them, and any fee or tax realities you'll face if you need to access cash from your investments. An experienced CDFA will also walk you through how your situation projects into the future, not just today.

Some family law attorneys are also CDFA certified; ask questions from your interview list. They tend to focus on business valuations rather than projecting whether budgets are reasonable and whether net worth will increase or decline.

> *What would everything be worth if it was all converted to cash, after all taxes, fees and penalties are paid.*

It might sound good now, but if you look at your situation based on today's patterns and you'll be going into a harmful situation a few years later, you need to revisit your settlement or figure out how to cut expenses or increase your income.

Taxes are inevitable and often a forgotten part of divorce settlements. We pay taxes on everything. Some in the present, some far off in the future. This impacts the actual value of any compensation.

Peter and Jenny have three considerable assets:

1. Their house
2. A 401k
3. A Brokerage Investment Account.

Each is estimated to be worth $650,000. They own the house with no mortgage. Peter wants to keep the brokerage account and half of his 401k. Jenny would get the house and the other half of the 401k. They each have $975,000.

Seems fair, no?

Well, Jenny would get the house with no liquidity, and when she sells it, she will have sales costs of 8 to 10 percent while also being taxed on anything she makes over $250,000 on the sale. Say she sells the house next year for $660,000.

Jenny pays $66,000 to sell the home in fees, needed maintenance, advertising and real estate charges. Since there is no mortgage, she now has $594,000. They paid $118,000 for the home years ago, we subtract that to get her gain. Now she has $476,000. Because this is greater than the individual capital gain allowed of $250,000, she will be taxed on everything over that at 15%. Jenny needs to pay 15 percent capital gains of $33,900 on the $226,000.

After selling the house Jenny will walk away with $560,200 (Her profit of $594,000 less the taxes of $33,900.) She does have the 401k, but she can't access that money without paying a 10 percent penalty and taxes. When she accesses it, she will pay taxes on all the $325,000 as though it was earned income. So her portion is $91,000 less in a 28 percent tax bracket. $325,000 less 28 percent is $234,000.

Jenny has $560,200 and $234,000, totaling $794,200.

Peter has $650,000 in the brokerage account. Since all the taxes are paid annually and he told his broker to make sure all of the gains were realized before it was valued so there aren't any outstanding taxes, his investment is worth $650,000, it is completely liquid (remember, he can convert it to cash and use it at any time) and any taxes in the future are based on the performance of the investment. He is not carrying forward a tax liability.

Peter will owe taxes on the 401k when he withdraws it. He is in a lower tax bracket than Jenny, so estimating his taxes on the 401k when he accesses it are 22 percent, his $325,000 less $71,500 is worth $253,500.

Jenny is receiving closer to $794,200, not the $975,000 she thought. Peter has $903,500 after taxes—$109,300 more than Jenny. Yikes.

You understand assets, personal versus marital property, liquidity, and taxes. Now what?

It's time to divide things. Where do you start?

Beware, and be aware, of this:

Frequently, I'll have someone come to me with the property settlement proposed by their attorney or their spouse's attorney, and it looks like this: [29]

29 Only the first page of each settlement scenario is shown for illustration.

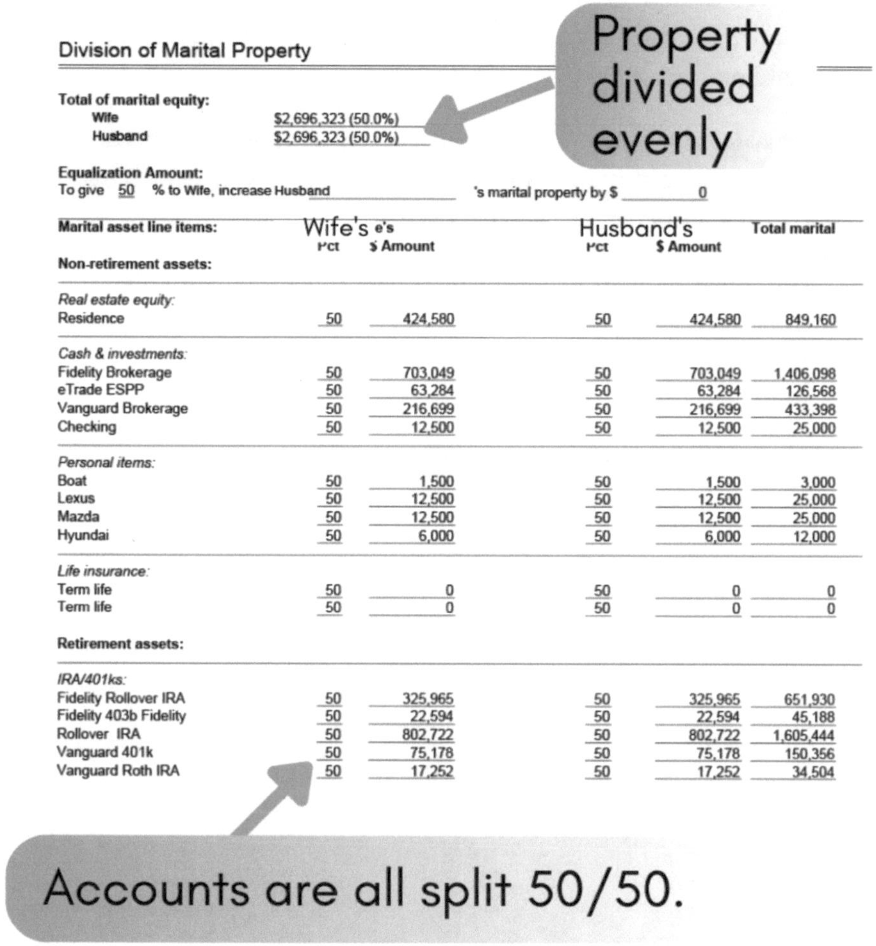

Division of Marital Property

Total of marital equity:

Wife	$2,696,323 (50.0%)
Husband	$2,696,323 (50.0%)

Equalization Amount:

To give 50 % to Wife, increase Husband 's marital property by $ 0

Marital asset line items:	Wife's Pct	Wife's $ Amount	Husband's Pct	Husband's $ Amount	Total marital
Non-retirement assets:					
Real estate equity:					
Residence	50	424,580	50	424,580	849,160
Cash & investments:					
Fidelity Brokerage	50	703,049	50	703,049	1,406,098
eTrade ESPP	50	63,284	50	63,284	126,568
Vanguard Brokerage	50	216,699	50	216,699	433,398
Checking	50	12,500	50	12,500	25,000
Personal items:					
Boat	50	1,500	50	1,500	3,000
Lexus	50	12,500	50	12,500	25,000
Mazda	50	12,500	50	12,500	25,000
Hyundai	50	6,000	50	6,000	12,000
Life insurance:					
Term life	50	0	50	0	0
Term life	50	0	50	0	0
Retirement assets:					
IRA/401ks:					
Fidelity Rollover IRA	50	325,965	50	325,965	651,930
Fidelity 403b Fidelity	50	22,594	50	22,594	45,188
Rollover IRA	50	802,722	50	802,722	1,605,444
Vanguard 401k	50	75,178	50	75,178	150,356
Vanguard Roth IRA	50	17,252	50	17,252	34,504

The property is divided evenly, but results in paying for QDROs (Qualified Domestic Relations Order) at $600 or more each. QDROs the legal documents needed to divide an Employee Retirement Income Security Act of 1974 (ERISA) account. Some of these accounts are Traditional, Cash Balance, or Money Purchase Defined Benefit Plans and some are Defined Contribution plans like Traditional, 401 (k), and Profit Sharing.

There are non-Erisa plans like state and local retirement systems that may have their own rules about whether they will allow division of the benefits.

Translation: you can't just split a retirement account because you want to, and some you cannot divide at all. If you can, it requires another legal document, the QDRO.

The case I refer to as an example had 19 QDROs involved, none of which were considered in the division of assets. The attorney had also divided assets that couldn't be split in two, like cars and term life policies.

And then we start to dig a little deeper. A similar settlement, when you consider taxes, might look like this:

Marital Property Division on an After-Tax Basis

This report presents an educated guess of the marital property on an after-tax basis.

1. Key tax rates used

	Marginal Tax Rate at Retirement	Capital Gains Rate Currently
Wife		
Federal:	12.00	0.00
State:	4.95	4.95
Husband		
Federal:	22.00	18.80
State:	4.95	4.95

After tax property is NOT even

2. Marital Property Division on an After-Tax Basis:

Wife	$2,429,271 (53.7%)
Husband	$2,091,290 (46.3%)

3. Marital Property After-Tax Detail

Description	(a) Pre-tax Marital Equity	(b) % Kept	Wife's % Paid In Tax	Wife's After Tax Equity (a*b*(1-c))	Husband's % Kept	Husband's % Paid In Tax	(g) Husband's After Tax Equity (a*e*(1-f))
Real Estate							
Residence	849,160	50	1.64	417,617	50	7.87	391,166
Total Real Estate				417,617			391,166
Cash & Investments							
Fidelity Brokerage	1,406,098	50	4.95	668,248	50	23.75	536,075
eTrade ESPP	126,568	50	4.95	60,151	50	23.75	48,254
Vanguard Brokerage	433,398	50	4.95	205,972	50	23.75	165,233
Checking	25,000	50	4.95	11,881	50	23.75	9,531
Total Cash & Investments				946,252			759,093
Personal Items							
Boat	3,000	50	0.00	1,500	50	0.00	1,500
Lexus	25,000	50	0.00	12,500	50	0.00	12,500
Mazda	25,00	50	0.00	12,500	50	0.00	12,500
Hyundai	12,00	50	0.00	6,000	50	0.00	6,000
Total Personal Items				32,500			32,500

Accounts are split 50/50.

WHOA! What?

Not only would they have to pay for multiple QDROs (over $11,000 in additional fees in the real case), but the wife would receive $337,981 more than the husband, even though their intent was to split assets evenly.

Yep. This happens when we don't look at a settlement from all perspectives. In this case, Joanie is in a much lower tax bracket, and we anticipate this will remain.

And they've each left 401k's at prior employers instead of rolling them over into Individual Retirement Accounts (IRAs). Because of that, they'll need to pay for a Qualified Domestic Relations Order (QDRO) for each divided account, which will cost them much more than transferring the assets to an IRA first.

Now, look at the identical accounts divided, taking taxes and QDROs into account:

Property divided evenly

Division of Marital Property

Total of marital equity:

Wife $2,696,323 (50.0%)

Husband $2,696,323 (50.0%)

Equalization Amount:

To give 50 % to wife, increase husband 's marital property by $ 0

Marital asset line items:	Wife's Pct	Wife's $ Amount	Husband's Pct	Husband's $ Amount	Total marital
Non-retirement assets:					
Real estate equity:					
Wilmette residence	50	424,580	50	424,580	849,160
Cash & investments:					
Fidelity Brokerage (Joint)	95	1,330,475	5	75,623	1,406,098
eTrade ESPP (Jeff)	0	0	100	126,568	126,568
Vanguard Brokerage (Joint)	42	183,398	58	250,000	433,398
Checking	50	12,500	50	12,500	25,000
Personal items:					
Boat	0	0	100	3,000	3,000
Lexus	0	0	100	25,000	25,000
Mazda	100	25,000	0	0	25,000
Hyundai	50	6,000	50	6,000	12,000
Life insurance:					
Term life wife	100	0	0	0	0
Term life husband	0	0	100	0	0
Retirement assets:					
IRA/401ks:					
Fidelity Rollover IRA (wife)	100	651,930	0	0	651,930
Fidelity 403b (wife) Fidelity	100	45,188	0	0	45,188
Rollover IRA (husband)	0	0	100	1,605,444	1,605,444
Vanguard 401k (husband)	0	0	100	150,356	150,356
Vanguard Roth IRA (Joint)	50	17,252	50	17,252	34,504

Accounts are not all split 50/50.

They won't need any QDROs. In their case, my rearranging the way their accounts were divided saved significantly more than they paid me to look at their settlement. I mention this because people can be hesitant to spend the money to engage another professional, however doing so often more than pays for itself. And because QDROs can take months to settle, they could finalize everything sooner by eliminating most of the QDROs their attorney had proposed.

START BY GATHERING ALL YOUR INFORMATION ABOUT WHAT YOU OWN

If you're working with a CDFA, they will be able to help you with this. We give our clients a form to fill out that prompts them through the various categories. We can use this information in our software to produce other asset division options that let our clients see the tax ramifications and impact on their long-term net worth.

If you'd like a sample to work with, contact the office at info@bridgingllc.com, and we'll send it to you. Ask for the *Asset and Liability Worksheet.* I firmly believe in including all the information you have about all your accounts, even if they aren't joint or marital assets. That way, there isn't any confusion about an account not being included. We might keep it in the settlement agreement showing that the separate account was discussed and was to remain the respective property of one of the spouses.

Each person should keep their own individual property. This includes things like gifts, inheritances, and personal items. Sometimes people inquire about what was a gift such as a wedding ring. That was considered a gift before marriage. Did it come in a box with a bow? Was it presented at a special event, like the birth of a child or an anniversary? That's a gift. If it was too big to put in a box but was given as a gift, like a car, it is not marital property. Maybe that had a bow on it too. It's a gift.

Make note: That ring, car, or whatever the item in question is, like everything else, is only worth what someone will pay for it.

There can be some bitterness at times that one party "got away with" thousands of dollars worth of jewelry when, if sold, it would be worth a fraction of that.

How accurately does this need to be done?

You want to have a good idea of the value of each investment or item, but don't make yourself crazy updating it or trying to have everything valued on the same date. When you finalize your accounts at the end of your process, you will pick one date to value everything and revise the numbers on your settlement spreadsheet to reflect the actual values.

HOW DO DEBTS FIT IN?

Debts are significant because they can impact a considerable portion of a couple's assets. In a divorce, dividing these debts between the two parties fairly and equitably is essential. What you owe is divided between the two parties, just as what you own is. This includes things like credit card debt, loans, and mortgages.

There are a few twists to that sentiment that debt should be divided between the two parties. Debt can frequently be sticky, particularly if one party runs up credit debts or takes loans that the other wasn't aware of or disapproved of.

This wasn't my case, but I learned of it years ago. Beata and Sam appeared to be very well off. They vacationed with their family in exotic places regularly. They belonged to a local country club. Beata hadn't worked outside of the home for years. She was highly active in her community volunteering and never missed one of her kids' extracurricular activities.

Every so often, Sam would present Beata with some paperwork to sign, which she did and then didn't give it a second thought. He took care of the money, and she took care of the family. Imagine her surprise when Sam told her they had nothing and were hundreds of thousands of dollars in debt.

Their marriage didn't survive the fictional financial life they'd been leading. Sam was willing to take on all the debt after their divorce because he incurred it without her knowledge. Had they let the courts decide, this probably wouldn't have been the case.

Community property laws vary from state to state. Still, any debt incurred during the marriage is generally considered community property and is subject to division between the two parties.

There are other circumstances where debt follows one person. Student loans are the most overt and, in my opinion, a logical example of this. If one party gets the benefit of what the loan funded, in this case, an education that can't be separated from the human who received it, they also get the debt incurred financing it.

As debt is addressed in your divorce proceedings, it's also important to consider each party's ability to repay it. If someone agrees to take on half of the debt but only makes 20 percent of the income, they probably can't afford to pay the same amount. You can consider factors like each person's income and ability to pay the debt when deciding what to do.

In most cases, the best way to divide debts is to negotiate between the two parties for the best and most reasonable outcome. Consider structuring your agreement so that joint debt is paid out of assets when you finalize your divorce. This could involve one spouse taking on more debt in exchange for receiving more investments in the divorce. This gives each of you a clean slate to move forward in your financial lives.

No matter which method you use to divide debts in a divorce, it is crucial to ensure that you are fair and equitable in your division. With the help of an experienced divorce professional, you can ensure that your debts are divided in a way that is best for both parties involved.

After the information is gathered and account values attached, take a breath.

Look at all of the things on your list and make sure you understand them. What type of account is it? Is it liquid or not? If not, what are the rules about accessing it?

Use this next section primarily as a reference. Likely, most of it doesn't apply to you. Make yourself familiar with the things that apply and note any questions about each asset category so you can get the information you need to make good decisions.

This is by no means a comprehensive list. It is pretty basic, so if you find that some of the things you own as property or investments are omitted here—you guessed it—get some help. You want the best information you can gather. Google is your friend, but sometimes going down that rabbit hole can be maddening and more confusing. A professional who can answer your questions about the nature of the account might be the answer. In the case of company-sponsored retirement accounts, you may need to be tenacious. If a good bit of your assets are in these accounts, it's worthwhile to dig deep and ensure you have a complete understanding of how they work and what limitations exist on those funds. Not doing this can be the most expensive mistake you ever make; I speak from experience. Expensive experience. I'll share that story in a bit.

CHAPTER 18 | DO THE WORK

- Put together a list of all of your assets, including the account numbers (or the last 4 digits), so they are readily identifiable.
    - A CDFA can help you value things like a business, or connect you with an expert who can if it's extremely complicated.
- Put together a list of any debts, including credit cards, even if you pay them off every month, include bank and account number (or last 4 digits).
- If you have questions about what is or is not marital, ask your attorney or a CDFA. (There may be times when an asset is both. Property tracing may be required to get good figures.)

CHAPTER 18 | RESULTS

> Do you know what you have and what you owe? This is the starting place to divide your assets.

- You will understand your assets and liabilities and what you need to consider to assign an actual value to them, like taxes and penalties.
- You'll know that the simple "put it in two columns and divide everything in half" may not be the best solution.

CHAPTER 18 | **HIGHLIGHTS**

- Assets are what you own that is valuable to someone else.
- Liabilities are what you owe.
- Both assets and liabilities can be considered marital or individual.
- Liquidity is how quickly you can or can't convert to cash.
- Taxes impact all finances and settlements.

CHAPTER 19

A Toolbox for Your Practical & Financial Shit

It's not about 'what can I accomplish?' but 'what do I want to accomplish?' Paradigm shift.
—Brené Brown

WITH THE RIGHT TOOLS and the right mindset, you can accomplish what you want to accomplish, not what you think you have to settle for. Don't settle! You're better than that. Here are a handful of resources to take with you on your journey.

BUDGETING

Budgeting sounds daunting, but when done correctly, it can set you up for a strong start to your next chapter in life. Often just the word makes people sweat. Try to think of it as knowing where your money is going so you can make good decisions. Here are some popular tools you can use to understand and prioritize where your money is going, look at the spending by category, like food, healthcare, or entertainment, and see how you're spending in one category relative to another. Is more than you think going to carry-out or travel? Is less than you think going to savings or an emergency fund?

When you understand what your expenses are to meet different standards of living, you will be able to make decisions about your settlement options. Can you live on the numbers you're discussing? Is it feasible for you to get a job that will make up any difference, or ultimately cover your expenses?

- You Need a Budget
- Albert
- Mint
- Goodbudget™

If you'd like to access our eMoney-based client websites to help you organize your finances throughout and after your divorce, send an email to info@bridgingdivorcesolutions.com, and we'll get you set up.

Prefer a spreadsheet? You can use this to download an excel spreadsheet to put your expenses together.

FINANCIAL DOCUMENT LIST

Here's a list of the financial documents you may be required to produce. What applies to you depends on the complexity of your financial situation and the method of divorce (your state or attorney may have different requirements).

BRIDGING DIVORCE SOLUTIONS

DOCUMENT LIST

- If Financial Affidavits have already been completed, provide copies
- Fully Completed Client Data Sheets with Post-Divorce Budget estimates for each party
- 3 years of tax returns with all supporting schedules and W-2s
- Last 3 month's statements on all investment accounts
- Last 3 month's statements for all bank accounts, checking, and/or savings
- Most recent three statements from any employee retirement plan, pension, or deferred comp plan
- Most recent statement on any Employee Stock Option, Employee Stock Purchase Plan, or Restricted Stock accounts.
- Most recent mortgage statement
- Most recent pay stubs for each party
- Last 3 months' statements for any and all credit cards with balances.
- Copies of most recent statements for any outstanding loans.
- Policy statements or information on any and all Life Insurance, Annuities, or Cash Value Insurance
- Social Security Estimate statements for both parties. These are available at www.SSA.gov
- For any businesses owned, a full Profit and Loss Statement and Balance Sheet for the current and previous 2 years (complete books may be required)
- For all autos owned - who holds the title, VIN numbers, and current mileage on vehicles
- Credit reports for both parties from www.AnnualCreditReport.com, www.CreditKarma.com, or other

2601 Broad Street, Suite 3 Chattanooga TN 37408. o| 844-306-0166. f|423.690.8111.

www.brendabridges.com. www.bridgingdivorcesolutions.com

CHILD SUPPORT AND SPOUSAL SUPPORT CALCULATORS

There are multiple online calculators available to get an idea of what child support and spousal support calculations may be in your area. Use these with caution unless they are provided by a government resource. They may be misleading or inaccurate.

FAMILY LAW SOFTWARE (FLS)

FLS reports are explicitly developed for divorcing couples to look at their finances, budgets, and settlements comprehensively. They're beneficial in seeing the impact of asset division and spousal and child support before and after taxes, but they can also project the financial impact of those decisions far into the future. Answering whether you will be OK can help confirm that an agreement is workable or point out areas that need addressing.

Family Law Software is not designed for personal use; you can engage a CDFA professional to work with you to run your reports and provide a thorough assessment of your financial case.

I use standard reports when working with my clients on their financial agreements. If you're interested in seeing a sample of these reports, go to the Appendix.

- Budget Report—spending for each party
- Child Support and Spousal Maintenance Summary
- Support Impact—the impact of child support and spousal maintenance on both parties' after-tax incomes
- Projected Net Income After Expenses and Taxes

- Five-Year Projection—key income, expense, and tax results projected for years, 1, 2, 3, 4, and 5
- Division of Marital Property—each item of property, its current value, and who is keeping it. It also shows totals for each property type
- Marital Property Division on an After-Tax Basis—an educated guess of the marital property on an after-tax basis
- Net Worth Spreadsheet—how much each party will have in the future based on the illustrated agreement
- Projected Net Worth—for 30 years
- Summary Totals Spreadsheet—income vs. assets and debt for each person for 30 years

If your professional doesn't have access to FLS, we are happy to coordinate with them to provide you with this information, so you're as informed as possible when working on your case.

DTour.life is a user-friendly portal that helps you organize your finances and work on your parenting plan in the same place. It can also communicate with your professional team, keeping things private, separate from other communications, and streamlined.

COMING SOON!

Email us at info@bridgingdivorcesolutions.com if you'd like to receive the workbook companion guide to ***Oh $h*t! I'm Getting Divorced***: *The Guide to Keeping Your Dollars and Dignity.*

CONCLUSION

Revisit Your *Why*

MY COMMITMENT TO KNOWING why I'm doing things crystalized with Simon Sinek's TED Talk. (Link is in the footnote below.[30])

Understanding the purpose behind your actions is essential for getting where you want to go in life. Knowing **why** you are doing something gives focus, motivation, and a sense of meaning.

Without a strong sense of purpose, you may go through the motions or, even worse, be swept into someone else's wake without feeling connected to your decisions. You may also need support to stay attentive to your goals to avoid becoming distracted or disheartened when faced with challenges or setbacks.

On the other hand, when you have a clear *why* behind your actions, you are better equipped to navigate obstacles and persevere when things aren't going smoothly. You feel more connected and directed to achieve your goals when guided by your *why*.

Knowing why you are doing something allows you to align your actions with your values and pursue meaningful objectives that bring you joy and satisfaction. So take a moment to reflect on your own *why*—it might be the key to unlocking your more positive future.

30 Sinek, Simon. 2010. "How Great Leaders Inspire Action." www.ted.com. May 4, 2010. https://www.ted.com/talks/simon_sinek_how_great_leaders_inspire_action/comments.

THANK YOU

TO MY SIBLINGS AND THEIR PARTNERS, Pam and Ray, Gail and Mike, Eddie and Leah, thank you for being my unwavering source of strength and lifeline during my darkest hours. I couldn't have made it without you. With love and gratitude. Y'all mean the world to me. (I can say that now that we all live in the South.)

To my friends, Robinn, Beth, Susie, and Marita, with profound gratitude and appreciation for your love and support when I needed it the most. Your presence, kind words, and open hearts helped me feel normal and loved, even when I felt broken and alone. You were there to remind me of my worth when I felt lost. You are remarkable human beings, and I love you more than words can express.

To my person Pat: you're the yang to my yin. You've shown me patience, love, and understanding. You've been there every step of the way—from encouraging me to try new things to patiently listening (or talking me down) when my emotions take over. You remind me that relationships don't need to be complicated to be fulfilling.

All we need is love and a little bit of grace. Thanks for being my partner in all things.

To all of my clients; past, present and future.

You trust me to help you move through this process, make it to the other side and on to your better life. Thank you. I know divorce is a really hard thing and I am dedicated to making it better for you, your families and your finances.

GLOSSARY

Affidavit
Written statement of facts you swear to be accurate, signed in front of a notary public.

Alimony (See Spousal Support)

Alternative Dispute Resolution (ADR)
Various methods to resolve conflicts and disputes between parties without going to court. ADR methods include Collaborative Process, negotiation, mediation, and arbitration techniques that encourage communication and goal-based decision-making between conflicting parties. ADR aims to find a mutually acceptable resolution that satisfies all parties involved.

Amicable Divorce
Type of divorce where both parties agree to end their marriage peacefully and cooperatively, without the need for litigation or contentious court battles. In an amicable divorce, the couple works together to reach a mutually acceptable agreement on issues such as property division, child custody, and spousal support. This approach often involves mediation or other forms of alternative dispute resolution to help the couple reach an agreement that works for both parties. Amicable divorces can be less stressful, time-consuming, and costly than traditional litigated divorces, and they can help preserve relationships between ex-spouses and children.

Annulment
Occurs when a court declares a marriage or domestic partnership not legally valid for allowed reasons, like age at the time of marriage, prior existing marriage, fraud, and force.

Asset
Something you own with value. Think of it as something you could sell to someone else.

Attorney
Legal professional licensed to practice law and provide legal advice and representation to clients. Attorneys may specialize in various areas of the law, such as criminal defense, family law, corporate law, or intellectual property law. They are responsible for representing their clients in court proceedings, negotiating on their behalf, drafting legal documents, and providing guidance on legal matters. Attorneys are also bound by ethical guidelines and must uphold professional standards of conduct when working with clients.

Business Valuation Specialist
Someone who specializes in determining the value of a business. They use different methods to assess a business's financial health, assets, liabilities, and potential to determine its fair market value. In divorce, they are hired to objectively assess a company's worth. Business valuation specialists usually have accounting, finance, or economics backgrounds and may hold certifications such as the Certified Valuation Analyst (CVA) designation.

Certified Divorce Coach® (CDC)
Trained professional who provides emotional, practical, and strategic support to individuals going through the divorce process. They help clients navigate the complex legal, financial, and emotional aspects. The role of a Certified Divorce Coach is to provide guidance, educa-

tion, and support so clients can make informed decisions. They work one-on-one or in group settings and may collaborate with other professionals such as lawyers, mediators, or financial planners to ensure that their clients receive comprehensive support. A Certified Divorce Coach completes a training program covering divorce law, mediation, communication skills, and coaching techniques.

Certified Divorce Financial Analyst® (CDFA)
Professional who helps couples through a divorce make fair and informed decisions about their money. They know about taxes, dividing assets, and the future impact of financial decisions. To become a CDFA, you have to be exam certified. The Institute for Divorce Financial Analysts (IDFA) offers this certification.

Child Support
Payments that one divorced parent makes to the custodial parent to cover the children's basic living expenses, such as food, housing, and clothing. These court-ordered payments are mandatory and determined by the formula (guideline) in the state of the minor child's residence.

COBRA
Consolidated Omnibus Budget Reconciliation Act. It is a federal law that allows individuals to continue to receive health insurance coverage under their employer's plan after they leave their job or experience certain life events, such as divorce or the death of a spouse. The COBRA law requires employers to offer continuation coverage for a limited period to an uninsured divorced spouse for thirty-six months. Individuals who elect COBRA coverage are responsible for paying the total cost of the insurance premiums themselves, plus an additional administrative fee. COBRA can be expensive but can provide a critical safety net for those who might otherwise lose access to health insurance due to divorce.

Cohabitation
The act of living together and having a sexual relationship without being married.

Collaborative Process
Method of divorcing by working together toward identified goals. The parties are supported by a team of professionals, usually two attorneys, a divorce coach (CDC) and a financial neutral (CDFA). Professionals provide direction and support, and all meetings are conducted privately. Participants sign a "participation agreement" committing to the process. If they leave the Collaborative Process to pursue litigation, the parties must start with new professionals.

Common Law Marriage
Legal union between two people who have not obtained a marriage license or had a formal ceremony but live together and hold themselves out as being married. In states that recognize common law marriage, the couple is considered legally married in the eyes of the law. The requirements for establishing a common law marriage can vary by state. Generally, to establish a common law marriage, both partners must be of legal age and capacity to enter into a marriage contract, live together in a committed relationship for a certain time period (often several years), and hold themselves out as being married to others.

Community Property
Legal concept that applies to certain types of property married couples acquire. Under community property laws, most assets and debts acquired during the marriage are considered jointly owned by both spouses, *regardless of which spouse earned or incurred them.* This means that each spouse has an equal ownership interest in the property and is typically entitled to an equal share of the property's value if the couple divorces or one spouse dies. Community property laws do

not apply to all types of assets; gifts and inheritances may be separate property. Rules regarding community property can vary by state.

Court Order

Legal document issued by a judge or court official that commands or authorizes a specific action, such as requiring someone to appear in court, pay a fine, or refrain from certain activities. It is enforceable by law, and the failure to comply with the terms of the court order can lead to fines or imprisonment.

Custody

Right and responsibility of caring for someone or something, typically a child or property. In the context of family law, custody often refers to the legal determination of who has physical and/or legal control over a minor child, including decisions related to their upbringing and well-being. This can include sole custody, joint custody, or shared custody arrangements.

Joint custody, both parents of a minor child share the responsibility for making important decisions about the child's upbringing, such as education, healthcare, and religious practices. Joint custody may also involve shared physical custody, meaning that the child spends significant time with both parents. Joint custody arrangements can vary widely depending on the needs and circumstances of each family.

Legal custody is used in family law to describe the authority and responsibility for making important decisions about a child's upbringing, such as those related to education, healthcare, religion, and other aspects of their welfare. A parent with legal custody has the right to make these decisions on behalf of their child and is responsible for ensuring that the child's best interests are taken into account. *Legal custody can be held solely by one parent or can be shared jointly between both parents*, depending on the specific circumstances of each case.

Shared, also known as **joint physical custody**, the child spends significant and roughly equal amounts of time with both parents. This can involve alternating weeks or weekends or any other schedule that works best for the family. Shared custody can be a good option for families who want to ensure that both parents have an ongoing and active role in their child's life after a divorce or separation.

Sole custody, one parent has the legal and physical custody of the child, and is solely responsible for making decisions about their upbringing. The parent with sole custody has full decision-making authority over important matters, such as education, healthcare, and religion, without needing to consult with the other parent. This type of custody arrangement is usually awarded in cases where one parent is deemed unfit or unable to provide proper care for the child, or if there are issues such as abuse, neglect, or domestic violence in the family. However, in some cases, parents may agree to sole custody voluntarily if they believe it's in the best interest of their child.

Physical refers to the right of a parent to have their child physically present with them. In child custody arrangements, physical custody determines where the child will live and who will provide day-to-day care. When one parent has physical custody, they are responsible for providing a home for the child and meeting their daily needs, such as food, clothing, and shelter. The other parent may have visitation rights or parenting time with the child. Physical custody can be awarded solely to one parent (sole physical custody) or shared between both parents (joint physical custody).

Decree

A court order that resolves a legal issue or dispute. Typically issued by a judge after a hearing or trial, it has the force of law. Decrees can cover a wide range of legal matters, such as divorce, child custody, property division, alimony, and child support. Once a decree is issued, it becomes binding on all parties involved in the case. Failure to comply with the terms of a decree can result in penalties or enforcement actions by the court. In some cases, decrees can be modified if there are significant changes in circumstances that warrant it.

Defendant

The person accused of committing wrongdoing. They are the party against whom an action or lawsuit is brought, and they are required to defend themselves against the allegations made by the plaintiff. Even when a couple is divorcing amicably or out of court, they are often required to name a plaintiff and defendant.

Deposition

Legal proceeding in which a witness gives sworn testimony outside of court. It is typically conducted as part of the discovery process prior to trial, and it allows both parties in a lawsuit to gather information and evidence from witnesses. During a deposition, the witness is asked questions by attorneys representing each side, and their answers are recorded by a court reporter or videographer. The witness must answer truthfully under penalty of perjury, and their testimony can be used as evidence in court. Depositions are often an important tool for building a case or preparing for trial.

Discovery

Process by which parties gather evidence and information from each other and from third parties. It is part of the pretrial phase of litigation, and it can include methods such as interrogatories (written questions that must be answered under oath), requests for the production of documents or other physical evidence, depositions (sworn testimony given outside of court), and requests for admission (requests that the other party admits or deny certain facts). The goal of discovery is to ensure that both sides have access to all relevant information so that they can build their cases effectively. Discovery can be a lengthy and complex process; it is often crucial to the outcome of a case.

Dissolution of Marriage (DMA)

Legal term for ending a marriage or marital union. It is commonly known as divorce. The method of dissolution of a marriage involves various legal and practical steps; these may include filing a petition for divorce in court, serving notice on the other spouse, dividing property and debts, determining child custody and support arrangements (if applicable), and finalizing the divorce decree. The specific requirements and procedures for obtaining a dissolution of marriage vary by state.

Dissipation of Marital Funds

Legal term that refers to the improper or wasteful use of marital assets by one spouse during a marriage, either in anticipation of a divorce or without the knowledge or consent of the other spouse.

Examples can include spending money on gambling, drugs, extramarital affairs, or unnecessary expenses unrelated to family needs. Dissipation can also occur when one spouse intentionally depletes assets to reduce the amount available for division during property distribution in a divorce settlement. The specific rules and standards for determining whether dissipation has occurred vary by state. Generally, they involve looking at the timing and purpose of expenditures, whether both spouses knew and benefited from the expenditure, and whether it was consistent with past spending patterns. If dissipation is found to have occurred, it may affect how marital property is divided in a divorce settlement and can result in an unequal distribution of assets.

Divorce

The legal process by which a marriage is ended (marriage contract dissolved). Depending on the jurisdiction, divorce may require that one party prove fault (such as adultery or cruelty) or it may be granted on a no-fault basis. Issues such as property division, spousal support, child custody, and child support must also be resolved during the divorce process. In some cases, these issues can be resolved through Collaborative Process or mediation outside of court. It must be finalized by a court proceeding.

Divorce Coach (see Certified Divorce Coach)

Guideline

Recommendations or instructions intended to help individuals achieve a specific goal or objective. Following guidelines can help ensure that individuals are acting in accordance with established standards and can improve outcomes for all parties involved. Guideline formulas are used in some states to determine child support and spousal support (alimony). *Note that guidelines are not always mandatory and may need to be adapted to meet the unique needs of each situation.*

Equitable Distribution

Legal term that divides marital property and debts between spouses in a divorce settlement. Under equitable distribution, assets and debts are divided fairly but *not necessarily equally*. The goal is to ensure that each spouse receives a fair share of the marital property based on their individual financial needs, contributions to the marriage (both financial and non-financial), and union length. Equitable distribution can include any assets or debts acquired during the marriage, including real estate, bank accounts, retirement accounts, investments, and personal property. Specific rules for equitable distribution vary by state.

Executive Compensation

Remuneration and benefits given to executives at companies, usually as incentives for their performance and business decisions. In addition to salary and bonuses, it can include stock options, and other forms of rewards. It can also include benefits such as medical insurance, car allowances, retirement plans, and more. Identifying and distributing executive compensation in divorce can require a greater degree of investigation and more creative calculations than traditional income. Some executive compensation structures do not allow division; this may significantly impact the separation of assets in divorce.

Family Law

Deals with family-related issues and domestic relationships such as marriage, adoption, child custody, divorce, and other related matters. It also covers issues like spousal support, paternity suits, alimony payments, and more. Family law aims to protect the rights of all parties involved in family disputes while ensuring that resolution is in the best interests of those involved.

Family Law Software (FLS)

Financial planning software specific to divorce. Includes calculations for child support, spousal support, asset division, income, and net worth projects before and after taxes, for example.

Financial Affidavit

Legal document that provides detailed information about an individual's income, expenses, assets, and debts. Often used in family law cases to help determine issues related to financial support or property division issues. Financial affidavits provide a picture of an individual's financial situation so the court can make informed decisions based on the evidence presented. The specific requirements for a financial affidavit can vary by jurisdiction but generally require full disclosure of all relevant financial information under oath.

Forensic Accountant

An accounting professional who investigates financial disputes. They use their expertise to analyze financial data and transactions, identify irregularities, trace funds, and assets through complex transactions, and identify fraudulent activity.

Guardian ad Litem (GAL)
A court-appointed advocate who represents the best interests of a child in divorce proceedings. They investigate, interview witnesses, and make recommendations to the court regarding custody, visitation, placement, and other matters.

Interrogatories
Written questions one party in a legal case sends to the other to gather information relevant to the case. They're a formal part of the pretrial discovery processes and cover facts, witnesses, evidence, and legal arguments. The receiving party must answer truthfully under penalty of perjury. Interrogatories are used in civil cases to gather information and build a case.

Joint Custody (see Custody)

Joint Property
Items of value (assets) owned by both parties in a marriage.

Kitchen Table
An informal and non-adversarial method of dispute resolution, often used in family law cases. The parties involved agree on the issues on their own. The term "kitchen table" suggests casual and friendly, as if the parties were sitting around a kitchen table discussing their issues. This approach can be less stressful and more cost-effective than going to court, and can help preserve relationships and promote cooperation between parties.

Legal Separation

A court-approved arrangement in which a married couple lives separately and divides their assets and responsibilities, while remaining legally married. It outlines the rights and obligations of each party, including child custody, spousal support, and property division. Legal separation is often a precursor to divorce, and may be chosen for religious, financial, or personal reasons.

Liability

Legal responsibility for actions or debts that can result in consequences such as financial damages or legal remedies.

Lifestyle Analysis

A financial review to assess an individual's standard of living, expenses, and income. It involves examining financial records to identify spending patterns and estimate future expenses and income potential.

Litigation

The process of solving a disagreement through the legal system, usually in a court. It involves presenting arguments and evidence to a judge or jury in order to reach a decision.

Maintenance (See Spousal Support)

Marital Property (or Marital Assets)

Marital Settlement Agreement (MSA), also DMA

A legal document that outlines the terms of a divorce settlement, including property division, spousal and child support, and custody arrangements. It's negotiated by both parties with their attorneys and must be approved by a judge to become legally binding.

Mediation
A way of resolving disputes with the help of a neutral third party. The mediator assists the parties in finding a mutually agreeable solution through exploration of possible solutions. The do not make decisions or impose solutions.

Memorandum of Understanding (MOU)
A non-binding document that outlines the terms and details of the divorce. In mediation, the MOU is provided to the attorney or document preparer to draft the DMA or MSA.

No-Fault Divorce
Divorce in which neither party has to prove that the other party caused the marriage breakdown. This approach avoids assigning blame or fault to one party.

Non-Custodial Parent
The parent who does not have physical custody of their child or children following a divorce or separation. Non-custodial parents typically still have legal rights and responsibilities related to their child. Non-custodial parents may also be involved in decisions regarding the child's upbringing.

Non-Marital Property
Assets or property owned by one spouse individually. Also known as separate property. Non-marital property can include assets acquired before the marriage, gifts or inheritances received during the marriage, or any property designated as distinct in a pre- or postnuptial agreement.

Orders of Protection (aka Restraining Orders)
Legal documents issued by a court that prohibit an individual from contacting or approaching another person. Typically used to protect

victims of domestic violence, stalking, or harassment. It may require the abuser to stay a certain distance from the victim and their home or workplace and prohibit communication with the victim. Violating can result in legal consequences such as fines or imprisonment. Protection orders can be temporary or permanent.

Parent-on-Duty (POD)
The parent caring for their child or children. This means that they are in charge of supervising, feeding, clothing, and meeting the needs of their children during a specific time. The idea behind "parent on duty" is to ensure an adult is present and responsible for the well-being of the children at all times.

Parenting Plan
A written agreement that outlines how parents will share the responsibilities of raising children after divorce. The plan typically includes where the child will live, visitation schedules, decision-making authority regarding the child's upbringing, and financial support arrangements. A well-drafted parenting plan can minimize conflict between parents and create stability for the child during a difficult time. It can also serve as a helpful reference point in future disputes or changes in circumstances.

Parenting Coordinator
Professional who works with separated or divorced parents to assist them in making decisions about their children's upbringing. The parenting coordinator acts as a neutral third party, helping the parents to communicate effectively, manage conflicts, and develop strategies for co-parenting. They may also provide education and support on child development, family dynamics, and conflict resolution issues. Parenting coordinators are typically appointed by a court or agreed upon by the parents themselves and may have the authority to make recommendations or decisions regarding parenting disputes. The

goal of working with a parenting coordinator is to promote cooperation between parents and ensure that the child's best interests are being met.

Petitioner or Plaintiff

Person who initiates a legal proceeding by filing a petition with a court. The petitioner is typically the party who brings the case to court and seeks relief or redress for some harm or injury. They are responsible for proving their case to the court. Even when a couple is divorcing amicably or out of court, they are often required to name a plaintiff and defendant.

Postnuptial Agreement

A legal contract entered into by a married couple after they are married. Like prenuptial agreements, postnuptial agreements typically address issues related to property division, spousal support, and other matters that may arise during a divorce or separation. Postnuptial agreements can be helpful for couples who want to clarify their financial rights and obligations before divorce or death.

Prenuptial Agreement (Premarital Agreement)

"Prenup" is a legal contract between two people before marriage. The purpose of a prenuptial agreement is to establish each spouse's financial and property rights in case the marriage ends in divorce or death. Prenups typically address property division, spousal support, and inheritance rights. They can be helpful for couples with significant assets, children from previous relationships, or other complex financial situations. Prenups are not only for wealthy individuals; anyone who wants to protect their assets and clarify their financial responsibilities can benefit from a prenuptial agreement.

Pro Se

Latin meaning "for oneself" or "on one's own behalf." In the divorce context, pro se refers to a person who represents themselves in court without the assistance of an attorney. They are responsible for preparing and filing their legal documents, conducting legal research, and presenting their cases to the judge or jury. Pro se representation is generally not recommended for complex or high-stakes cases; it can be difficult for non-lawyers to navigate the legal system effectively.

Respondent (see Defendant)

Restraining Order (see Order of Protection)

QDRO (Qualified Domestic Relations Order)
A court order which creates or recognizes the existence of an alternate payee's right to receive or assigns to an alternate payee the right to receive all or a portion of the benefits payable to a participant under a retirement plan. It can also be used in other family law matters, such as division of assets and payment of alimony or child support.

Separate Property
Any asset or debt acquired prior to marriage, as a result of inheritance or gift, or obtained during marriage through the sale of separate property. This type of property is not subject to division in case of divorce and remains with the spouse who owns it. NOTE: something can move from separate property to joint property (or marital) if it's put in a joint account or title.

Settlement Agreement
The written contract between spouses or former spouses that sets out the terms and conditions of their separation, dissolution, or divorce. It is typically used to resolve matters related to child custody and support, spousal support, division of property and debts, alimony, and other related matters.

Split Custody (see Custody)

Spousal Benefits

The rights, privileges, and advantages that are given to married couples under the laws of their particular jurisdiction. Such benefits may include tax exemptions, rights to inherit property without a will, social security spousal survivor benefits, health care coverage, beneficiary status on pensions, rights pertaining to child custody and support, and more

Spousal Support (Alimony, Maintenance)

Court-ordered payment that one spouse has to make to their ex-spouse during or after divorce. Its purpose is to provide financial assistance to the spouse with less income. One of the thoughts behind spousal support is the right of divorced parties to live according to their accustomed standard of living. The duration of alimony payments varies based on factors such as income and length of the marriage.

Temporary spousal support during the divorce process to help the lower-earning spouse meet their financial needs while the legal proceedings are ongoing. This is a short-term solution until a more permanent arrangement can be made.

Rehabilitative spousal support is awarded when one spouse requires financial assistance to obtain education or training that will enable them to become self-supporting. This support is often given for a fixed period and may be contingent upon the recipient meeting certain requirements, such as completing a degree program or obtaining a certain level of employment.

Permanent spousal support is less common than temporary or rehabilitative support and is awarded in cases where one spouse has been out of the workforce for an extended time or has limited earning potential due to age, health, or disability. In these situations, the court may order ongoing financial assistance from one spouse to the other indefinitely. ("Permanent" may mean to traditional retirement age vs. lifetime.)

Statement of Net Worth

Written document that lists the assets, liabilities, and respective net worth of each spouse. The document can be used to determine how much financial support one spouse may be required to provide the other or resolve property disputes.

Stipulation

An agreement between two parties in a legal case that resolves some or all of the issues between them without requiring a trial. Both sides agree to certain facts, waiving certain rights, or agreeing to certain orders from the court. Stipulations are typically submitted in writing and signed by both parties before being entered into the court record.

Tax Effect

The sum of all taxes resulting from the transaction or event, including those collected by the government and paid by the taxpayer. For example, when looking at a settlement, the tax effect would calculate the value to each party before taxes are paid and the estimated value after taxes are paid on the assets.

Transferring

When children go from one home to another, and the parent on duty responsibility is switched, we often refer to transferring as how the child transitions from one household to another.

Uncontested Divorce

Both parties agree to all the terms of the divorce. In an uncontested divorce, both spouses agree to the division of property, child custody and support, alimony, and other issues without going to trial. It is a streamlined process in which the parties often need only file the divorce petition and related documents, as well as a settlement agreement, with the court. After review, a judge can grant the divorce without a hearing.

Visitation

Legal right of a non-custodial parent to spend time with their child. Visitation rights can also be granted to other family members, such as grandparents, in certain situations. Visitation schedules are typically determined through court agreements or mediation and can include specific dates, times, and locations for visitation. The purpose of visitation is to promote the relationship between the non-custodial parent and child.

Vocational Assessment

A series of tests, interviews, and other activities designed to assess the skills, abilities, and interests of an individual. The process helps employers and individuals understand what type of job would best suit the individual's strengths, interests, and career goals. In divorce, it may help determine the party's earning potential or need for additional training. Vocational assessments may include aptitude tests, personality profiles, interviews with career counselors or mentors, work samples, and more.

"What If" Scenarios

Options in looking at settlements with different financial scenarios. Variables may change, like how assets are divided or how much support is paid. The "what if" scenarios show the end results of those changes so parties can compare options in context to what they mean.

APPENDIX

In the following, you will find a set of reports based on a hypothetical settlement for Mark and Mary. Using a CDFA to work through your settlement options will give you information like this to see what your settlement will mean for you in reality.

In a real case, this is where we would start. This scenario presents several problems.

While reviewing the reports, we see that Mary is spending more than her income will support, her net worth continues to decline even though she received half of the marital assets, and she's got to use her savings to survive.

She either needs to earn more or spend less.

Mark continues on his income trajectory and is able to sustain the support payments and increase his net worth substantially over the years.

If you'd like to see alternative solutions to this case, or how your situation looks five or thirty years down the road, email us at info@bridgingdivorcesolutions.com. We'll be happy to help you look at your options.

Financial Analysis

Party A: Mary Smith
Party B: Mark Jones
Date: 03/19/2023 - 12:55pm
Case: 000 001 Mary Smith Petitioner, Mark Jones Respondent

Contact & Background Information

Mary Smith
Birth Date: 06/08/1984
State where Mary Smith lives: IL
Address: 345 6th Street, Chicago, IL 60000
Phone: (777)555-1212

Mark Jones
Birth Date: 02/25/1983
State where Mark Jones lives: IL
Address: 123 Second Street, Garden Apartment, Chicago, IL 0000
Phone: (888) 555-1212

Children

Janie
Birth Date: 09/15/2012
Janie is a child of this relationship.
Janie is young enough to be eligible for child support.
Mary Smith will claim the tax exemption.
Janie will be a tax exemption until 21.

Jimmy
Birth Date: 12/07/2018
Jimmy is a child of this relationship.
Jimmy is young enough to be eligible for child support.
Mary Smith will claim the tax exemption.
Jimmy will be a tax exemption until 21.

Julie
Birth Date: 03/05/2009
Julie is a child of this relationship.
Julie is young enough to be eligible for child support.
Mary Smith will claim the tax exemption.
Julie will be a tax exemption until 21.

Prepared by: Brenda Bridges, MAT, CDFAÂ®, RICPÂ®, Mediator, IACP, IDFA
Bridging Divorce Solutions LLC
2601 Broad Street
Suite 3
Chattanooga, TN 37408
Phone: 844-366-0166
E-mail: brenda@bridgingllc.com

Brenda Bridges is NOT AN ATTORNEY AND DOES NOT PROVIDE LEGAL ADVICE. Divorce financial planning is a fee-only process that does not involve investment advice or securities or insurance transactions.

Budget Report—Spending for Each Party

Budget Report for 2023

This report shows Mary's and Mark's income, taxes, and expenses, including both alimony and child support income and expenses.

	Mary Monthly	Mark Monthly
Income		
Great Designs Inc	$6,050.00	$0.00
ABC Inc	0.00	25,735.67
Bonuses	416.00	6,300.00
Total Wage and Wage-Like Income	$6,466.00	$32,035.67
Rental Income		
1000 First Street	$619.00	$0.00
Total Rental Income	$619.00	$0.00
Support Received		
Child Support Received	$3,188.00	$0.00
Alimony Received	$4,771.00	$0.00
Total Support Received	$7,959.00	$0.00
TOTAL INCOME	**$15,044.00**	**$32,035.67**

Mortgage Payments		
1000 First Street	$0.00	$0.00
Total Mortgage Payments	$0.00	$0.00
Household		
Rent	$3,400.00	$1,650.00
Homeowners' Insurance	200.00	0.00
Renters' Insurance	100.00	30.00
Real Estate Tax	225.00	0.00
Cable TV	30.00	30.00
Internet Access	100.00	60.00
Phone	200.00	75.00
Household Maintenance	100.00	0.00
Furniture & Appliance	50.00	0.00
Household Supplies	27.00	18.00
Maid/Cleaning Service	150.00	200.00
Lawn Service	140.00	0.00
Trash Removal	0.00	15.00
Utilities - Electricity	100.00	100.00
Utilities - Gas/Propane Heat	120.00	50.00
Utilities - Water/Sewer	12.00	0.00
Other Household	100.00 (1)	0.00
Living Expenses - Household	$5,054.00	$2,228.00

Budget Report for 2023

	Mary Monthly	Mark Monthly
Transportation		
Car Payments	$375.00	$0.00
Car Insurance	87.00	59.00
Car Gasoline/Oil	100.00	150.00
Car Maintenance and Repair	100.00	150.00
Car License/Stickers	148.00	0.00
Tolls	50.00	0.00
Public/Alt. Transportation	50.00	150.00
Living Expenses - Transportation	$910.00	$509.00
Child		
Child Care - Sitters	$500.00	$0.00
Child Clothing/School Uniforms	200.00	150.00
Child Education Books/Fees	50.00	0.00
Child Education Room & Board	300.00	0.00
Child Grooming	50.00	25.00
Child Groceries	0.00	200.00
Child Medical Doctor	150.00	0.00
Child Medical Dentist	50.00	0.00
Child Medical Optical	50.00	0.00
Child Medical Medication	100.00	0.00
Child Vacation	300.00	150.00
Child Camp	100.00	0.00
Child Entertainment	200.00	100.00
Child Tutors	1,000.00	0.00
Other Child	200.00	50.00
Living Expenses - Child	$3,250.00	$675.00
Personal		
Cell Phone	$122.00	$87.00
Clothes	500.00	100.00
Dry Cleaning	50.00	30.00
Charitable	50.00	0.00
Dues/Clubs	75.00	0.00
Entertainment	400.00	700.00
Food/Groceries	2,000.00	800.00
Gifts	50.00	200.00
Hair	300.00	75.00
Laundry	100.00	50.00
Legal and Accounting	250.00	29.00
Pets	50.00	0.00
Subscriptions, Books	100.00	0.00
Therapist/Counselor	200.00	300.00
Travel	500.00	200.00
Living Expenses - Personal	$4,747.00	$2,571.00

Budget Report for 2023

	Mary Monthly	Mark Monthly
Health and Medical		
Health Insurance	$500.00	$388.00
Dental Insurance	50.00	148.00
Medical/Doctor	100.00	100.00
Dental	50.00	100.00
Drug & Prescription	100.00	0.00
Optical	50.00	0.00
Orthodontist	100.00	0.00
Living Expenses - Health and Medical	$950.00	$736.00
Total Living Expenses	$14,911.00	$6,719.00
Deductible IRA/401k Contrib		
Great Graphics Inc 401k	$182.00	$0.00
ABC Inc 401k	0.00	1,287.00
Total Deductible IRA/401k Contrib	$182.00	$1,287.00
Insurance Premiums		
Term life	$127.00	$0.00
National Life	0.00	450.00
Whole Life	0.00	600.00
Total Insurance Premiums	$127.00	$1,050.00
Debts		
Chase Visa	$0.00	$0.00
Captial One MC - Joint	$0.00	$0.00
Chase Visa Prime	$0.00	$0.00
Macy's Card	$0.00	$0.00
TJ Maxx Card	$0.00	$0.00
Delta Amex - Joint	$0.00	$0.00
AMEX	$0.00	$0.00
Total Debt Payments	$0.00	$0.00
Support Paid		
Child Support Paid	$0.00	$3,188.00
Alimony Paid	0.00	4,771.00
Total Support Paid	$0.00	$7,959.00
TOTAL EXPENSES	**$15,220.00**	**$17,015.00**

Taxes		
Federal Taxes	$67.08	$7,828.33
Social Security & Medicare	$494.67	$1,430.50
State Taxes (estimate only)	$0.00	$0.00
Local Wage Tax	$0.00	$0.00
TOTAL TAXES	**$561.75**	**$9,258.83**

Budget Report for 2023

	Mary Monthly	Mark Monthly
Total Income	$15,044.00	$32,035.67
Minus Total Expenses	(15,220.00)	(17,015.00)
Minus Total Taxes	(561.75)	(9,258.83)
BUDGET NET INCOME	$(737.75)	$5,761.83

Mary does not have enough money to meet her expenses. She wil either need to cut costs or bring in more income.

Child Support and Spousal Maintenance Summary.

Child Support & Alimony Summary

Child support and alimony summary report for Mary Smith and Mark Jones.

Child Support

$38,256	Annual child support payment in current year by Mark
$3,188	Monthly payment.
10%	Percent of Mark's gross income (current year).

Alimony

$57,252	Annual payment in current year by Mark
$4,771	Monthly payment.

Child Support + Alimony

25%	Percent of Mark's gross income (current year).

Filing Statuses

Filing Status in Year of Divorce:

Mary: Head of Household

Mark: Single

Filing Status After Divorce:

Mary: Head of Household

Mark: Single

Exemptions

Number of Exemptions (including self) for Mary: 4

Number of Exemptions (including self) for Mark: 1

Support Impact—Impact of Child Support and Spousal Maintenance on Both Parties' After-Tax Incomes.

Support Impact Report - Monthly - 2023 Actual

	Mary	Mark
1. Income	7,085	32,036
2. Child Support	3,188	(3,188)
3. Alimony	4,771	(4,771)
4. Inc aft suppt (lns 1 to 3)	15,044	24,077
5. Total taxes & mand exp	562	9,259
6. Inc After Taxes (4-5)	14,482	14,818
7. % of Combined	49	51
8. Living Expenses	15,220	9,056
9. Net Aft Tax & Exp	(738)	5,762

Mary is running a deficit each month.

This graph shows the impact of child support, spousal support, and taxes on each party.

- The two bars at the left show each party's gross income.
- The two bars at the right show each party's gross income after child support, alimony, and taxes.
- Typically, the bars on the right will be closer together, showing the equalizing effect of support and taxes.

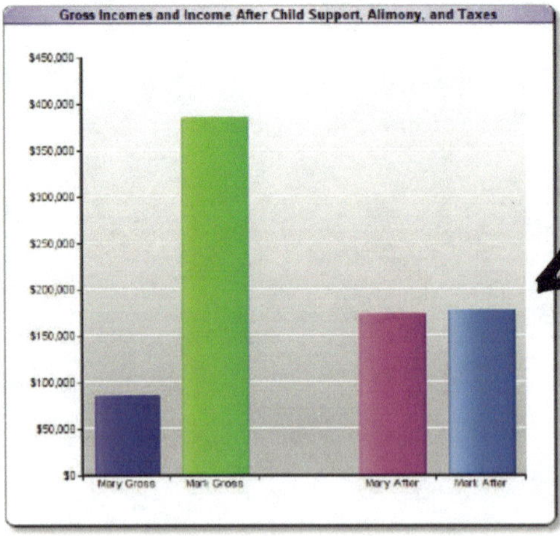

They've divided their property relatively evenly.

Projected Net Income After Expenses and Taxes.

Projected Net Income After Expenses and Taxes

Projected Net Income After Expenses and Taxes for Mary Smith and Mark Jones for 20 years.

	Mary	Mark
2023	($ 8,853)	$ 69,142
2024	($ 14,229)	$ 78,276
2025	($ 13,257)	$ 88,108
2026	($ 22,263)	$ 98,641
2027	($ 32,653)	$ 114,140
2028	($ 39,018)	$ 127,746
2029	($ 45,728)	$ 140,805
2030	($ 55,243)	$ 157,568
2031	($ 47,882)	$ 180,887
2032	($ 54,157)	$ 197,294

	Mary	Mark
2033	($ 60,781)	$ 214,814
2034	($ 83,553)	$ 247,916
2035	($ 135,712)	$ 311,266
2036	($ 154,307)	$ 334,085
2037	($ 196,448)	$ 380,399
2038	($ 220,768)	$ 407,418
2039	($ 247,539)	$ 436,356
2040	($ 279,148)	$ 467,351
2041	($ 311,810)	$ 500,551
2042	($ 347,700)	$ 536,103

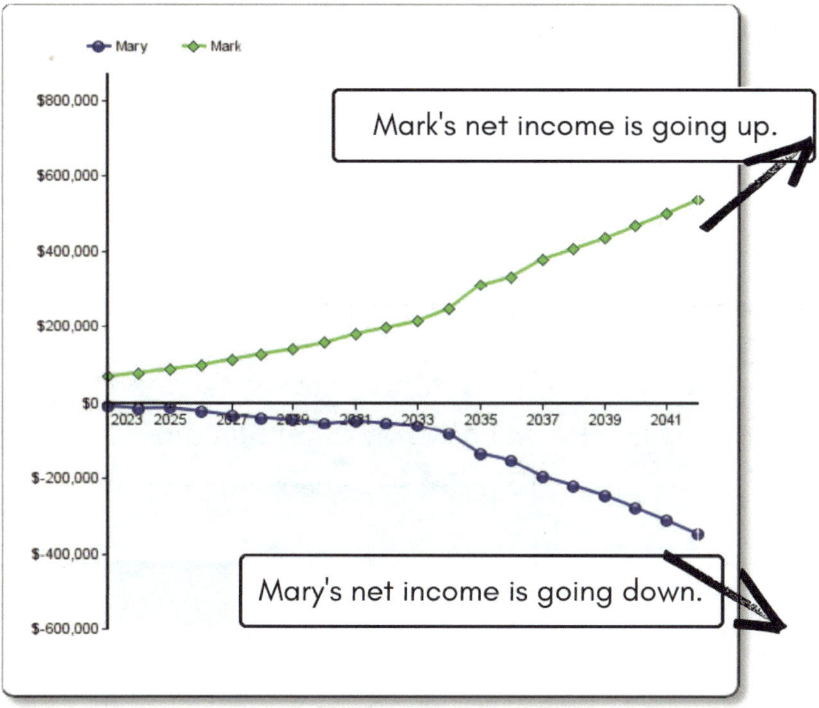

Spreadsheet for Net Income After Expenses and Taxes

Spreadsheet for Net Income After Expenses and Taxes (Annual)

Mary Spreadsheet for Net Income After Expenses and Taxes

Year	Age	Wages & Salary	Non-Wage Income	Real Est. Income	Child Support	Alimony Received	Total Income	Living Expenses	IRA/401k Contribs	Life Ins. Premiums	Acc Debt Interest
2023	39	72,600	4,992	7,428	38,256	57,252	180,528	178,932	2,184	1,524	0
2024	40	76,593	4,992	8,666	38,256	57,252	185,759	188,775	2,184	1,524	0
2025	41	80,806	4,992	9,971	38,256	57,252	191,277	192,484	2,184	1,524	0
2026	42	85,250	4,992	11,348	38,256	57,252	197,098	202,361	2,184	1,524	0
2027	43	89,939	4,992	12,802	34,008	57,252	198,993	213,491	2,184	1,524	0
2028	44	94,886	4,992	14,335	32,592	57,252	204,057	223,660	2,184	1,524	0
2029	45	100,105	4,992	15,952	32,592	57,252	210,893	235,970	2,184	1,524	0
2030	46	105,611	4,992	17,658	29,853	57,252	215,366	248,952	2,184	1,524	0
2031	47	111,420	4,992	19,458	21,636	57,252	214,758	238,696	2,184	1,524	0
2032	48	117,548	4,992	21,358	21,636	57,252	222,786	251,819	2,184	1,524	0
2033	49	124,013	4,992	23,361	21,636	57,252	231,254	265,677	2,184	1,524	0
2034	50	130,834	4,992	25,475	21,636	42,939	225,876	280,290	2,184	1,524	0
2035	51	138,030	4,992	27,705	21,636	0	192,363	295,694	2,184	1,524	1,786
2036	52	145,622	4,992	30,058	21,636	0	202,308	311,960	2,184	1,524	12,512
2037	53	153,631	4,992	32,540	0	0	191,163	329,122	2,184	1,524	24,725
2038	54	162,081	4,992	35,159	0	0	202,232	347,216	2,184	1,524	40,310
2039	55	170,995	4,992	37,921	0	0	213,908	366,316	2,184	1,524	57,840
2040	56	180,400	4,992	40,836	0	0	226,228	386,473	2,184	1,524	77,512
2041	57	190,322	4,992	43,911	0	0	239,225	407,729	2,184	1,524	99,730
2042	58	200,790	4,992	47,155	[illegible]	0	252,937	430,146	2,184	1,524	124,562

We can see when Mary's suport payments end she will have even less income to meet expenses

Year	Age	Total Expenses	Pre-tax Cash flow	Federal Inc Tax	FICA / Soc Sec	Total Taxes	Net After Exp&Tax
2023	39	182,640	(2,112)	805	5,936	6,741	(8,853)
2024	40	192,483	(6,724)	1,264	6,241	7,505	(14,229)
2025	41	196,192	(4,915)	1,779	6,563	8,342	(13,257)
2026	42	206,069	(8,971)	6,388	6,904	13,292	(22,263)
2027	43	217,199	(18,206)	7,185	7,262	14,447	(32,653)
2028	44	227,368	(23,311)	8,067	7,640	15,707	(39,018)
2029	45	239,678	(28,785)	8,903	8,040	16,943	(45,728)
2030	46	252,660	(37,294)	9,488	8,461	17,949	(55,243)
2031	47	242,404	(27,646)	11,330	8,906	20,236	(47,882)
2032	48	255,527	(32,741)	12,042	9,374	21,416	(54,157)
2033	49	269,385	(38,131)	12,781	9,869	22,650	(60,781)
2034	50	283,998	(58,122)	15,041	10,390	25,431	(83,553)
2035	51	301,188	(108,825)	15,946	10,941	26,887	(135,712)
2036	52	328,180	(125,872)	16,913	11,522	28,435	(154,307)
2037	53	357,555	(166,392)	17,921	12,135	30,056	(196,448)
2038	54	391,234	(189,002)	18,984	12,782	31,766	(220,768)
2039	55	427,864	(213,956)	20,120	13,463	33,583	(247,539)
2040	56	467,693	(241,465)	23,501	14,182	37,683	(279,148)
2041	57	511,167	(271,942)	24,927	14,941	39,868	(311,810)

Mary will continue to accrue a deficit, she'll need to dramatically cut back spending or make more money.

Mark Spreadsheet for Net Income After Expenses and Taxes

Year	Age	Wages & Salary	Non-Wage Income	Income on Accum Svg	Total Income	Living Expenses	IRA/401k Contribs	Life Ins. Premiums	Alimony Paid	Child Supt Pd	Total Expenses
2023	40	308,828	75,600	0	384,428	80,628	15,444	12,600	57,252	38,256	204,180
2024	41	325,814	75,600	2,073	403,487	85,065	15,444	12,600	57,252	38,256	208,617
2025	42	343,734	75,600	4,506	423,840	89,740	15,444	12,600	57,252	38,256	213,292
2026	43	362,639	75,600	7,329	445,568	94,679	15,444	12,600	57,252	38,256	218,231
2027	44	382,584	75,600	10,581	468,765	99,886	15,444	12,600	57,252	34,008	219,190
2028	45	403,626	75,600	14,430	493,656	105,378	15,444	12,600	57,252	32,592	223,266
2029	46	425,825	75,600	18,837	520,262	111,174	15,444	12,600	57,252	32,592	229,062
2030	47	449,245	75,600	23,817	548,662	117,288	15,444	12,600	57,252	29,853	232,437
2031	48	473,953	75,600	29,496	579,049	123,736	15,444	12,600	57,252	21,636	230,668
2032	49	500,020	75,600	36,102	611,722	130,542	15,444	12,600	57,252	21,636	237,474
2033	50	527,521	75,600	43,464	646,585	137,726	15,444	12,600	57,252	21,636	244,658
2034	51	556,535	75,600	51,648	683,783	145,304	15,444	12,600	42,939	21,636	237,923
2035	52	587,144	75,600	61,152	723,896	153,288	15,444	12,600	0	21,636	202,968
2036	53	619,437	75,600	72,936	767,973	161,718	15,444	12,600	0	21,636	211,398
2037	54	653,506	75,600	85,875	814,981	170,617	15,444	12,600	0	0	198,661
2038	55	689,449	75,600	100,722	865,771	179,998	15,444	12,600	0	0	208,042
2039	56	727,369	75,600	116,973	919,942	189,900	15,444	12,600	0	0	217,944
2040	57	767,374	75,600	134,745	977,719	200,349	15,444	12,600	0	0	228,393
2041	58	809,580					15,444	12,600	0	0	239,412
2042	59	854,107					15,444	12,600	0	0	251,033

Mark's chart is split to fit the page

Mark Spreadsheet for Net Income After Expenses and Taxes

Year	Age	Pre-tax Cash flow	Federal Inc Tax	FICA / Soc Sec	Total Taxes	Net After Exp&Tax
2023	40	180,248	93,940	17,166	111,106	69,142
2024	41	194,870	98,481	18,113	116,594	78,276
2025	42	210,548	103,331	19,109	122,440	88,108
2026	43	227,337	108,535	20,161	128,696	98,641
2027	44	249,575	114,162	21,273	135,435	114,140
2028	45	270,390	120,201	22,443	142,644	127,746
2029	46	291,200	126,716	23,679	150,395	140,805
2030	47	316,225	133,675	24,982	158,657	157,568
2031	48	348,381	141,136	26,358	167,494	180,887
2032	49	374,248	149,146	27,808	176,954	197,294
2033	50	401,927	157,774	29,339	187,113	214,814
2034	51	445,860	166,990	30,954	197,944	247,916
2035	52	520,928	177,003	32,659	209,662	311,266
2036	53	556,575	188,035	34,455	222,490	334,085
2037	54	616,320	199,569	36,352	235,921	380,399
2038	55	657,729	211,959	38,352	250,311	407,418
2039	56	701,998	225,179	40,463	265,642	436,356
2040	57	749,326	239,285	42,690	281,975	467,351
2041	58	799,923	254,333	45,039	299,372	500,551
2042	59	854,009	270,388	47,518	317,906	536,103

Even after support payments Mark's net income continues to rise.

Five-Year Projection—Key Income, Expense, and Tax Results Projected for Years, 1, 2, 3, 4, and 5

Five Year Projection

Projections for Mary Smith and Mark Jones.

This table shows key income, expense and tax results projected for years, 1, 2, 3, 4, and 5. The graph below shows net worth projected for 20 years.

	# Years	1	2	3	4	5
	Year	2023	2024	2025	2026	2027
Total Income						
	Mary	$180,528	$185,759	$191,277	$197,098	$198,993
	Mark	*$384,428*	*$403,487*	*$423,840*	*$445,568*	*$468,765*
Total Expenses						
	Mary	$182,640	$192,483	$196,192	$206,069	$217,199
	Mark	*$204,180*	*$208,617*	*$213,292*	*$218,231*	*$219,190*
Total Taxes						
	Mary	$6,741	$7,505	$8,342	$13,292	$14,447
	Mark	*$111,106*	*$116,594*	*$122,440*	*$128,696*	*$135,435*
Net Income After Expenses and Taxes						
	Mary	($8,853)	($14,229)	($13,257)	($22,263)	($32,653)
	Mark	*$69,142*	*$78,276*	*$88,108*	*$98,641*	*$114,140*
Year-End Net Worth						
	Mary	$701,884	$732,724	$766,997	$793,064	$809,412
	Mark	*$771,676*	*$885,891*	*$1,014,323*	*$1,158,175*	*$1,322,944*

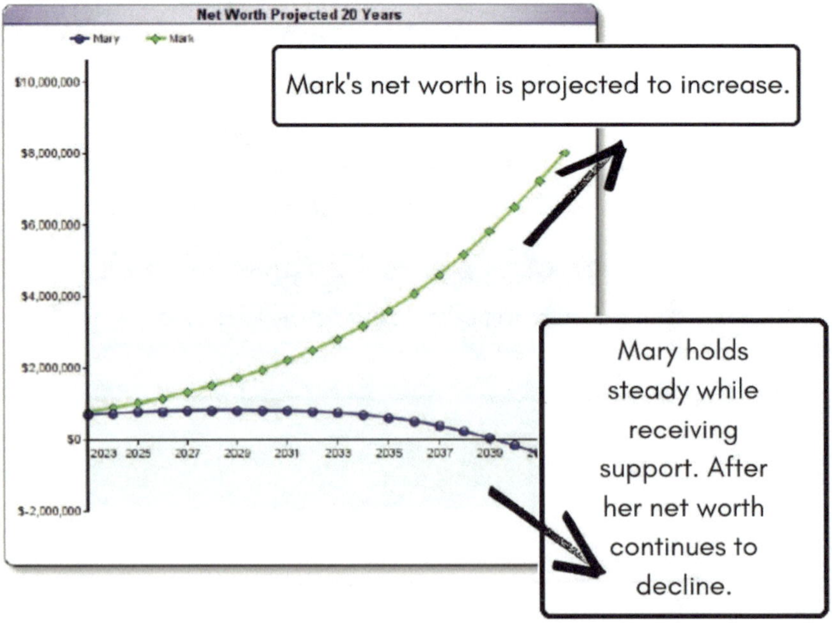

Division of Marital Property—Each Item of Property, Its Current Value, and Who Is Keeping It. It also Shows Totals for Each Property Type

Division of Marital Property

Property division report for Mary Smith and Mark Jones.

		Mary Amount	Mark Amount	Total Amount
Real Estate Equity				
1000 First Street		$153,000	$0	$153,000
Total Value	$475,000			
1st Mortgage	$322,000			
Marital Equity	$153,000			
Cash & Investments				
Cash-Equivalent Investments:				
Chase Checking		$2,500	$2,500	$5,000
Chase Premier Checking		$10,500	$0	$10,500
Chase Savings		$0	$18,000	$18,000
Bank of America		$0	$800	$800
American Funds Account		$34,400	$51,600	$86,000
Total Cash-Equivalent		$47,400	$72,900	$120,300
Other Investments:				
Apple		$124,770	$0	$124,770 est
Healthcare FSA		$8,127	$8,127	$16,254
ABC Inc.		$0	$14,821	$14,821
Total Other Investments		$132,897	$22,948	$155,845
Total Investments		$180,297	$95,848	$276,145
Businesses				
Business #1		--	--	$0
Cars and Personal Effects				
2009 Mazda CX-9		$12,995	$0	$12,995
2019 Escalade (1)		$0	$37,783	$37,783
Total Personal Items		$12,995	$37,783	$50,778
Life Insurance				
Term life (2)		$0	$0	$0
National Life (3)		$0	$22,300	$22,300
Whole Life		$0	$127,000	$127,000
Total Life Insurance		$0	$149,300	$149,300
Subtotal Non-Retirement		**$346,292**	**$282,931**	**$629,223**
IRA/401ks				
Stock Profit Sharing		$91,800	$112,200	$204,000
Great Graphics Inc 401k		$0	$10,605	$10,605
ABC Inc 401k		$0	$276,845	$276,845
Rollover IRA		$160,376	$13,946	$174,322
Total IRA/401ks		$252,176	$413,596	$665,772

Property division report for Mary Smith and Mark Jones.

	Mary Amount	Mark Amount	Total Amount
Defined Benefit Pensions			
TRS	$98,300	$0	$98,300
Total Pensions	$98,300	$0	$98,300
Subtotal Retirement	**$350,476**	**$413,596**	**$764,072**
Total Assets	**$696,768**	**$696,527**	**$1,393,295**
Debts			
Chase Visa	($10,000)	$0	($10,000)
Captial One MC - Joint	($752)	($752)	($1,503)
Chase Visa Prime	($462)	$0	($462)
Macy's Card	($255)	$0	($255)
TJ Maxx Card	($528)	$0	($528)
Delta Amex - Joint	($5,000)	($5,000)	($10,000)
AMEX	$0	($16,000)	($16,000)
Total Debt	($16,997)	($21,752)	($38,748)
Total Debts	**($16,997)**	**($21,752)**	**($38,748)**
Total Assets	**$696,768**	**$696,527**	**$1,393,295**
Total Debts	**($16,997)**	**($21,752)**	**($38,748)**
Total Marital Property	**$679,771**	**$674,775**	**$1,354,547**

	Mary Amount	Mark Amount
Property Settlements		
[2022]	$0	$0
Property Settlements	$0	$0
Total After Property Settlement	**$679,771**	**$674,775**

Children's Assets:

Cash & Investments

Other Investments:	
529	$168,000
Total Investments	$168,000
Total Children's Assets	**$168,000**

Note: "Total Amount" column may not add due to rounding.

Footnotes:

(1) 2019 Escalade - lease / no residual value

(2) Term life - premium information not supplied. beneficiary information needs to be confirmed.

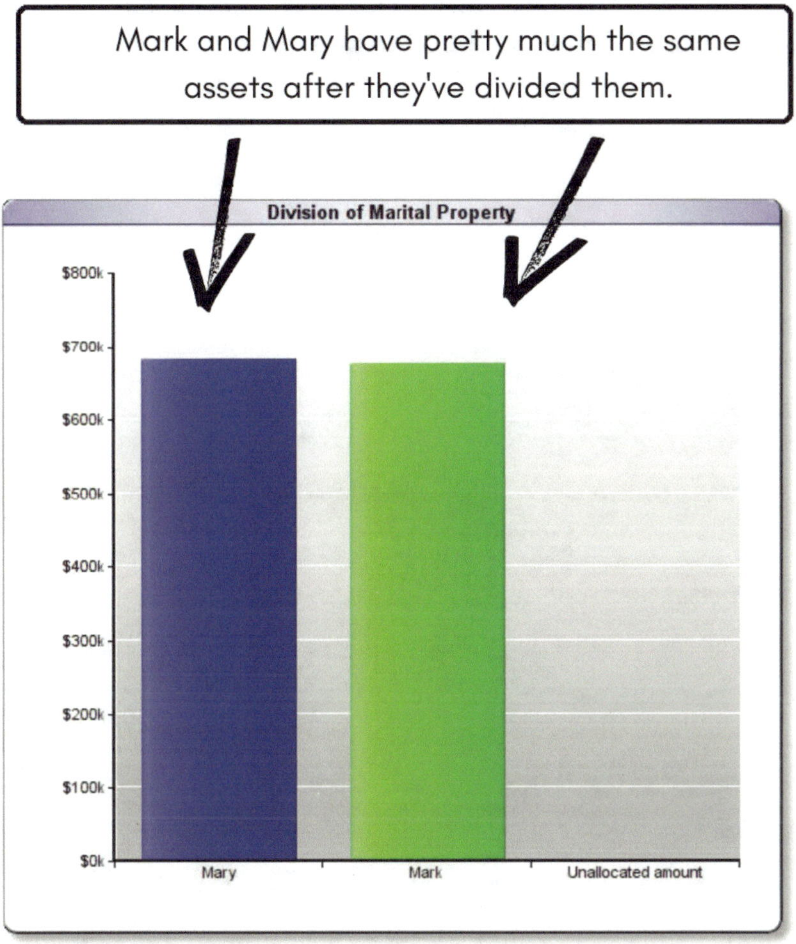
Mark and Mary have pretty much the same assets after they've divided them.
Division of Marital Property
$800k
$700k
$600k
$500k
$400k
$300k
$200k
$100k
$0k
Mary
Mark
Unallocated amount

Marital Property Division on an After-Tax Basis—An Educated Guess of the Marital Property On an After-Tax Basis

This report presents an educated guess of the marital property on an after-tax basis.

1. Key tax rates used

	Marginal Tax Rate at Retirement	Capital Gains Rate Currently
Mary		
Federal	12.00	0.00
State	4.95	4.95
Mark		
Federal	24.00	18.80
State	4.95	4.95

2. Marital Property Division on an After-Tax Basis and Property Settlement:

Mary	$ 589,806 (52.6%)
Mark	$ 532,275 (47.4%)

3. Marital Property After-Tax Detail

Description	(a) Pre-tax Marital Equity	(b) % Kept	(c) Mary % Paid In Tax	(d) After Tax Equity (a*b*(1-c))	(e) % Kept	(f) Mark % Paid In Tax	(g) After Tax Equity (a*e*(1-f))
Real Estate							
1000 First Street	153,000	100	14.14	131,366	0	0.00	0
Total Real Estate				131,366			0
Cash & Investments							
Chase Checking	5,000	50	4.95	2,376	50	23.75	1,906
Chase Premier Checking	10,500	100	4.95	9,980	0	0.00	0
Chase Savings	18,000	0	0.00	0	100	23.75	13,725
Apple	124,770	100	4.95	118,594	0	0.00	0
Bank of America	800	0	0.00	0	100	23.75	610
Healthcare FSA	16,254	50	4.95	7,725	50	23.75	6,197
529	168,000		0.00	0		0.00	0
ABC Inc.	14,821	0	0.00	0	100	23.75	11,301
American Funds Account	86,000	40	4.95	32,697	60	23.75	39,345
Total Cash & Investments				171,372			73,084
Businesses							
	0		0.00	0		0.00	0
Total Businesses				0			0

Description	(a) Pre-tax Marital Equity	(b) % Kept	(c) Mary % Paid In Tax	(d) After Tax Equity (a*b*(1-c))	(e) % Kept	(f) Mark % Paid In Tax	(g) After Tax Equity (a*e*(1-f))
Personal Items							
2009 Mazda CX-9	12,995	100	0.00	12,995	0	0.00	0
2019 Escalade	37,783	0	0.00	0	100	0.00	37,783
Total Personal Items				12,995			37,783
Life Insurance							
Term life	0	100	0.00	0	0	0.00	0
National Life	22,300	0	0.00	0	100	0.00	22,300
Whole Life	127,000	0	0.00	0	100	0.00	127,000
Total Life Insurance				0			149,300
IRA/401ks							
Stock Profit Sharing	204,000	45	16.95	76,240	55	28.95	79,718
Great Graphics Inc 401k	10,605	0	0.00	0	100	28.95	7,535
ABC Inc 401k	276,845	0	0.00	0	100	28.95	196,698
Rollover IRA	174,322	92	16.95	133,192	8	28.95	9,909
Total IRA/401ks				209,432			293,860
Defined Benefit Pension							
TRS	98,300	100	16.95	81,638	0	28.95	0
Total Defined Benefit Pension				81,638			0
Debts							
Chase Visa	10,000	100	0.00	10,000	0	0.00	0
Captial One MC - Joint	1,503	50	0.00	752	50	0.00	752
Chase Visa Prime	462	100	0.00	462	0	0.00	0
Macy's Card	255	100	0.00	255	0	0.00	0
TJ Maxx Card	528	100	0.00	528	0	0.00	0
Delta Amex - Joint	10,000	50	0.00	5,000	50	0.00	5,000
AMEX	16,000	0	0.00	0	100	0.00	16,000
Total Debts				16,997			21,752
Marital Property Division on an After-Tax Basis				589,806			532,275

Even though the division of assets looked pretty even, after we account for taxes Mary actually has a greater percentage.

Disclaimer: Not legal advice.

Bridging Divorce Solutions LLC Prepared by Brenda Bridges, MAT, CDFAÂ®, RICPÂ®, Mediator, IACP, IDFA (c) Family Law Software, Inc. v 25.01

Net Worth Spreadsheet—How Much Each Party Will Have In the Future, Based on the Illustrated Agreement

Net worth spreadsheet

Mary Net worth spreadsheet

Year	Age	Fin. assets	Equity in real est.	IRA/401k	Defined Benefit	Debt	Accum. savings	Net worth
2023	39	169,882	156,864	266,969	98,300	(3,126)	0	701,884
2024	40	153,134	186,990	282,502	100,649	(3,546)	0	732,724
2025	41	137,537	218,695	298,812	102,998	(4,040)	0	766,997
2026	42	111,345	252,064	315,937	105,347	(4,624)	0	793,064
2027	43	72,930	287,184	333,918	107,696	(5,311)	0	809,412
2028	44	27,027	324,149	352,797	110,045	(6,123)	0	820,890
2029	45	0	363,058	341,711	112,394	(7,081)	0	823,077
2030	46	0	404,016	280,151	114,743	(8,211)	0	803,694
2031	47	0	447,129	231,352	117,092	(9,545)	0	799,023
2032	48	0	492,514	165,219	119,441	(11,119)	0	779,050
2033	49	0	540,293	85,679	121,790	(12,976)	0	747,781
2034	50	0	590,593	0	124,139	(15,168)	(22,320)	690,239
2035	51	0	643,550	0	126,488	(17,756)	(156,394)	608,883
2036	52	0	699,304	0	128,837	(20,810)	(309,062)	511,264
2037	53	0	758,006	0	131,186	(24,414)	(503,872)	373,901
2038	54	0	819,816	0	133,535	(28,670)	(723,002)	214,674
2039	55	0	884,898		135,884	(33,695)	(968,902)	31,180
2040	56	0	953,428		138,233	(39,628)	(1,246,630)	(181,602)
2041	57	0	1,025,590		140,582	(46,634)	(1,557,020)	(424,487)
2042	58	0	1,101,582		142,931	(54,907)	(1,903,300)	(700,699)

Note: Numbers are all as of "end of year."

Mary is depleting her savings and starts to accumulate debt in her fifties.

Chart split to increase readability.

Mark Net worth spreadsheet

Year	Age	Fin. assets	Equity in real est.	IRA/401k	Accum. savings	Net worth
2023	40	95,848	0	449,719	69,142	771,676
2024	41	95,848	0	487,650	150,184	885,891
2025	42	95,848	0	527,477	244,299	1,014,323
2026	43	95,848	0	569,295	352,712	1,158,175
2027	44	95,848	0	613,205	480,960	1,322,944
2028	45	95,848	0	659,310	627,944	1,507,477
2029	46	95,848	0	707,719	793,867	1,711,901
	47	95,848	0	758,549	983,190	1,940,580
	48	95,848	0	811,921	1,203,405	2,200,880
	49	95,848	0	867,962	1,448,835	2,486,962
	50	95,848	0	926,804	1,721,602	2,800,749
	51	95,848	0	988,589	2,038,382	3,158,675
	52	95,848	0	1,053,462	2,431,183	3,592,448
	53	95,848	0	1,121,580	2,862,515	4,064,217
	54	95,848	0	1,193,104	3,357,415	4,598,582
	55	95,848	0	1,268,204	3,899,130	[illegible]
	56	95,848	0	1,347,058	4,491,451	[illegible]
	57	95,848	0	1,429,855	5,138,460	6,486,454
	58	95,848	0	1,516,791	5,844,549	7,221,804
	59	95,848	0	1,608,074	6,614,434	8,016,174

Mark's net worth and savings continue to grow.

Chart split to increase readability.

Summary Totals Spreadsheet—Income vs. Assets and Debt for Each Person for 30 Years

Summary Totals Spreadsheet

Mary Summary Totals Spreadsheet

Year	Age	INCOME Total Income	Total Expenses	Total Taxes	Net After Exp & Tax
2023	39	180,528	182,640	6,741	**(8,853)**
2024	40	185,759	192,483	7,505	**(14,229)**
2025	41	191,277	196,192	8,342	**(13,257)**
2026	42	197,098	206,069	13,292	**(22,263)**
2027	43	198,993	217,199	14,447	**(32,653)**
2028	44	204,057	227,368	15,707	**(39,018)**
2029	45	210,893	239,678	16,943	**(45,728)**
2030	46	215,366	252,660	17,949	**(55,243)**
2031	47	214,758	242,404	20,236	**(47,882)**
2032	48	222,786	255,527	21,416	**(54,157)**
2033	49	231,254	269,385	22,650	**(60,781)**
2034	50	225,876	283,998	25,431	**(83,553)**
2035	51	192,363	301,188	26,887	**(135,712)**
2036	52	202,308	328,180	28,435	**(154,307)**
2037	53	191,163			
2038	54	202,232			
2039	55	213,908			
2040	56	226,228			
2041	57	239,225			
2042	58	252,937			

Mary is deficit spending from year one.

ASSETS & DEBT Accum Savings	Fin Assets	Equity in Real Est.	IRA/401k	Other Assets/Debt	Net Worth
0	169,882	156,864	266,969	108,169	**701,884**
0	153,134	186,990	282,502	110,098	**732,724**
0	137,537	218,695	298,812	111,953	**766,997**
0	111,345	252,064	315,937	113,718	**793,064**
0	72,930	287,184	333,918	115,380	**809,412**
0	27,027	324,149	352,797	116,917	**820,890**
0	0	363,058	341,711	118,308	**823,077**
0	0	404,016	280,151	119,527	**803,694**
0	0	447,129	231,352	120,542	**799,023**
0	0	492,514	165,219	121,317	**779,050**
0	0	[illegible]	85,679	121,809	**747,781**
[illegible]	0	[illegible]	0	121,966	**690,239**
56,394)	0	[illegible]	0	121,727	**608,883**
09,062)	0	699,304	0	121,022	**511,264**
03,872)	0	758,006	0	119,767	**373,901**
23,002)	0	819,816	0	117,860	**214,674**
68,902)	0	884,898	0	115,184	**31,180**
46,630)	0	953,428	0	111,600	**(181,602)**
57,020)	0	1,025,590	0	106,943	**(424,487)**
03,300)	0	1,101,582	0	101,019	**(700,699)**

Mary has spent her 401k and is not saving anything for retirement.

Mark Summary Totals Spreadsheet

Mark's assets continue to grow, even when carrying debt.

		INCOME				
Year	Age	Total Income	Total Expenses	Total Taxes	**Net After Exp & Tax**	A Sa
2023	40	384,428	204,180	111,106	**69,142**	6
2024	41	403,487	208,617	116,594	**78,276**	15
2025	42	423,840	213,292	122,440	**88,108**	24
2026	43	445,568	218,231	128,696	**98,641**	35
2027	44	468,765	219,190	135,435	**114,140**	48
2028	45	493,656	223,266	142,644	**127,746**	62
2029	46	520,262	229,062	150,395	**140,805**	79
2030	47	548,662	232,437	158,657	**157,568**	98
2031	48	579,049	230,668	167,494	**180,887**	1,20
2032	49	611,722	237,474	176,954	**197,294**	1,44
2033	50	646,585	244,658	187,113	**214,814**	1,72
2034	51	683,783	237,923	197,944	**247,916**	2,03
2035	52	723,896	202,968	209,662	**311,266**	2,43
2036	53	767,973	211,398	222,490	**334,085**	2,86
2037	54	814,981	198,661	235,921	**380,399**	3,35
2038	55	865,771	208,042	250,311	**407,418**	3,89
2039	56	919,942	217,944	265,642	**436,356**	4,49
2040	57	977,719	228,393	281,975	**467,351**	5,13
2041	58	1,039,335	239,412	299,372	**500,551**	5,84
					536,103	6,61

ASSETS & DEBT					
Accum Savings	Fin Assets	Equity in Real Est.	IRA/401k	Other Assets/Debt	**Net Worth**
69,142	95,848	0	449,719	156,967	**771,676**
150,184	95,848	0	487,650	152,209	**885,891**
244,299	95,848	0	527,477	146,699	**1,014,323**
352,712	95,848	0	569,295	140,320	**1,158,175**
480,960	95,848	0	613,205	132,931	**1,322,944**
627,944	95,848	0	659,310	124,375	**1,507,477**
793,867	95,848	0	707,719	114,467	**1,711,901**
983,190	95,848	0	758,549	102,993	**1,940,580**
1,203,405	95,848	0	811,921	89,706	**2,200,880**
1,448,835	95,848	0	867,962	74,317	**2,486,962**
1,721,602	95,848	0	926,804	56,495	**2,800,749**
2,038,382	95,848	0	988,589	35,856	**3,158,675**
2,431,183	95,848	0	1,053,462	11,955	**3,592,448**
2,862,515	95,848	0	1,121,580	(15,726)	**4,064,217**
3,357,415	95,848	0	1,193,104	(47,785)	**4,598,582**
3,899,130	95,848	0	1,268,204	(84,912)	**5,178,270**
4,491,451	95,848	0	1,347,058	(127,910)	**5,806,447**
5,138,460	95,848	0	1,429,855	(177,709)	**6,486,454**
5,844,549	95,848	0	1,516,791	(235,384)	**7,221,804**
6,614,434	95,848	0	1,608,074	(302,182)	**8,016,174**

ICPA®, Mediator, IAC

CITATIONS

1. "Where Are You on the Divorce Stress Scale?" Psychology Today, Sussex Publishers, https://www.psychologytoday.com/us/blog/contemplating-divorce/201207/where-are-you-the-divorce-stress-scale.

2. Whitener, Svetlana. "Council Post: How Your Emotions Influence Your Decisions ." Forbes, Forbes Magazine, 12 Oct. 2022, https://www.forbes.com/sites/forbescoachescouncil/2018/05/09/how-your-emotions-influence-your-decisions/.

3. "Working with a CDFA." IDFA, https://institutedfa.com/learning-center/what-cdfa-professional/.

4. Squinx. "CDC Board of Standards." Certified Divorce Coach®, n.d. https://certifieddivorcecoach.com/cdc-board-of-standards/.

5. "The Healthy Journal - Gluten, Dairy, Sugar Free Recipes, Interviews and Health Articles," n.d. https://www.thehealthyjournal.com.

6. "The Healthy Journal - Gluten, Dairy, Sugar Free Recipes, Interviews and Health Articles," n.d. https://www.thehealthyjournal.com/faq/is-divorce-worse-than-death.

7. Mediation Plus® is used with permission of and credit to Smarter Divorce Solutions.

8. "Divorce Information & Articles | Lawyers.com." n.d. www.lawyers.com. Accessed March 24, 2023. https://www.lawyers.com/legal-info/family-law/divorce/.

9. Lang, Tyler. 2022. "Council Post: The Financial Impact of Divorce." Forbes. October 20, 2022. https://www.forbes.com/sites/forbesfinancecouncil/2022/10/20/the-financial-impact-of-divorce/.

10. Crail, Chauncey. 2022. "How Much Does a Divorce Cost in 2022? – Forbes Advisor." www.forbes.com. July 29, 2022. https://www.forbes.com/advisor/legal/divorce/how-much-does-divorce-cost/.

11. Michon, Kathleen, and Attorney. n.d. "How Much Will My Divorce Cost and How Long Will It Take?" www.nolo.com. https://www.nolo.com/legal-encyclopedia/ctp/cost-of-divorce.html.

12. Sember, Brette. 2022. "How Long Does a Divorce Take? – Forbes Advisor." Www.forbes.com. September 28, 2022. https://www.forbes.com/advisor/legal/divorce/how-long-does-divorce-take/.

13. Jimenez Law Firm. 2022. "Why Women Initiate Divorce | Understanding Female Initiated Divorce." The Jimenez Law Firm. June 22, 2022. https://www.thejimenezlawfirm.com/why-women-initiate-divorce-more-often-than-men.

14. "Women More Likely than Men to Initiate Divorces, but Not Non-Marital Breakups - American Sociological Association." 2022. American Sociological Association. September 28, 2022. https://www.asanet.org/women-more-likely-men-initiate-divorces-not-non-marital-breakups/.

15. "Child Support in the United States." 2023. Wikipedia. March 19, 2023. https://en.wikipedia.org/wiki/Child_support_in_the_United_States.

16. Heineig, Melissa. n.d. "No-Fault Divorce vs. Fault Divorce FAQ." www.nolo.com. Accessed March 24, 2023. https://

www.nolo.com/legal-encyclopedia/no-fault-divorce-vs-fault-divorce-faq.html#two.

17. Reuters Editorial. 2019. "Business & Financial News, U.S & International Breaking News | Reuters." Reuters. 2019. https://www.reuters.com/.

18. Hogan, Allie. 2020. "This Is When You'll Be Ready to Date Post-Divorce, Research Shows." Best Life. October 6, 2020. https://bestlifeonline.com/dating-after-divorce-survey/.

19. United States Government Accountability Office, "The Nation's Retirement System," 2017

20. Lin, I-Fen, and Susan Brown. 2020. "OUP Accepted Manuscript." Journals of Gerontology Series B: Psychological Sciences and Social Sciences. https://doi.org/10.1093/geronb/gbaa157.

21. "Francine Shapiro, Ph.D. | EMDR Institute – EYE MOVEMENT DESENSITIZATION and REPROCESSING THERAPY." 2019. emdr.com. 2019. https://www.emdr.com/francine-shapiro-ph-d/.

22. CDC. 2019. "FastStats - Marriage and Divorce." Centers for Disease Control and Prevention. 2019. https://www.cdc.gov/nchs/fastats/marriage-divorce.htm.

23. Stone, Lyman. 2021. "The Religious Marriage Paradox: Younger Marriage, Less Divorce." Institute for Family Studies. December 15, 2021. https://ifstudies.org/blog/the-religious-marriage-paradox-younger-marriage-less-divorce.

24. "Mindfulness for Your Health." 2021. NIH News in Health. June 1, 2021. https://newsinhealth.nih.gov/2021/06/mindfulness-your-health#:~:text=Health%20Benefits%20of%20Mindfulness&text=Mindfulness%2Dbased%20treatments%20have%20been.

25. Bernstein, Gabby. 2020. "How to Use the Abraham-Hicks Emotional Guidance Scale." Gabby Bernstein. February 2, 2020. https://gabbybernstein.com/emotional-guidance-scale-abraham-hicks/.

26. Early Childhood Learning & Knowledge Center. 2020. "The Importance of Schedules and Routines | ECLKC." Eclkc.ohs.acf.hhs.gov. June 1, 2020. https://eclkc.ohs.acf.hhs.gov/about-us/article/importance-schedules-routines.

27. Child support laws and expectations - US news & world report. (n.d.). Retrieved March 24, 2023, from https://money.usnews.com/money/personal-finance/family-finance/articles/child-support-laws-and-expectations

28. Deckard, Mallory. 2017. "Child Support and Deliberate Reduction of Income: What Can You Do?" Kahn, Dees, Donovan & Kahn, LLP. July 10, 2017. https://kddk.com/2017/07/10/child-support-and-deliberate-reduction-of-income-what-can-you-do/.

29. "Topic No. 452 Alimony and Separate Maintenance | Internal Revenue Service." n.d. www.irs.gov. https://www.irs.gov/taxtopics/tc452.

30. Only the first page of each settlement scenario is shown for illustration.

31. Sinek, Simon. 2010. "How Great Leaders Inspire Action." Www.ted.com. May 4, 2010. https://www.ted.com/talks/simon_sinek_how_great_leaders_inspire_action/comments.

Made in the USA
Monee, IL
13 July 2026

57083155R00190